Baseball History Research 101

A How-to Guide to Producing Factual,
Quality Work and Unearthing never-
before-presented Material

Brian McKenna

Contents

Introduction

Like many, I have been a baseball fan my entire life, since 1974 when I was eight years old. Being from Baltimore, I loved Brooks Robinson and always made my father sit on the third base side at Memorial Stadium to be near the hot corner. This was back in the days before mass computers when you bought your tickets at the gate closest to the seat you wanted.

I traded cards with friends, read all I could about the game and conversed with like-minded individuals. I even became a bit of a recluse during my teenage years as I cut pictures and articles from the newspapers, collected trading cards and did a host of other sorting, filing and reading to feed my passion. I dove into rotisserie baseball after a college professor introduced it to me. He was headed to Japan for the summer and wanted someone to manage his club in his absence.

When I turned thirty, I figured I knew enough that I could begin to write on the subject of baseball history. Problem was I didn't have a specific topic in mind. It took a couple years before I settled on one and then I began the research.

The first thing I learned was that I didn't know anything. Sure, I had read baseball for over twenty years by then but I never really connected everything and I have to admit I never really researched any subjects in great detail – I just grabbed what I saw at the bookstore and read it. There wasn't much deep thought to my process, just soaking in what others wrote.

The topic I chose for my first work was vast. I wanted to gather what I could about men whose baseball careers ended for reasons outside the norm – death, gambling, game-fixing, criminal activity, war, illness, dependency, lure of another sport, etc. or those otherwise forced out of the game. Seems straight forward but then I realized that my focus was merely on major leaguers. Plus, like many, I often just focused on the modern era. Well, that wouldn't do – baseball history is much more than that. I had to incorporate black baseball, international baseball – mainly Japan and Latin America, the minor leaguers, the nineteenth century game and female baseball. I did place one limit; I focused on professional players for the most part.

I didn't know enough in any of these areas to competently write anything. I had to bone-up on the material and I had to weave everything together in my mind. I started with biographical composites such as *The Ballplayers* and *Baseball: The Biographical Encyclopedia*. These were huge works but I had to start somewhere – the biggest works obviously contain the most widespread material. I read these and other tomes to get acquainted with the material. I needed to intertwine in my mind the eras, players, teams, championships and various nuances of the sport through the ages, at all levels of competition. I decided to memorize every World Series – the years, teams and winners. At least that was a start, a foundation to build from.

I quickly realized that secondary sources such as books were great but inadequate in and of themselves. First, they only present material that has already been researched. Second, many authors simply rehash what others have written before. I was finding errors – and a slew of them. Things just didn't match up when I put them on a timeline or juxtaposed them with other accrued data. Something was wrong.

Another thing that concerned me was that some of the things we've accepted as truths for decades weren't actually the case when I dove further into a subject – the whole issue of merely repeating and repeating the same material. These 'Baseball Myths,' as I like to call them, kept popping up. Even when someone thoroughly researched the topic and debunked a certain myth, people just didn't listen. How can you tell someone who has repeatedly heard that Ty Cobb was the devil that much of what they heard about him was inaccurate, skewed or presented with an author's agenda – which is much more prevalent that one realizes?

Some still believe Cobb actually killed someone and other stories which have been long ago debunked. The same goes for John Clarkson. He did not go insane and slay his wife. In a biography of him, I pulled up old newspapers and showed that his wife was at his funeral. Nonetheless, it's still repeated.

There are countless tidbits in baseball history that are repeated as truths but are nonetheless partially or wholly inaccurate. Such as, Walter Johnson did not pitch his entire career for lousy teams. In fact, from 1912 on the Senators were all-in-all fine nines through the end of his career. Even little things are mistakenly presented for effect. For example, a persistently story is repeated about a pitcher – Danny Friend – being called in from the clubhouse to play the outfield while wearing a bathrobe. The story seems funny but loses some of its appeal when I pulled up the article from the next day's newspaper and found that he was wearing one of the team's ulsters (an overcoat) instead.

Moreover, there is a persistent story about a clash between John McGraw and Clark Griffith whereby McGraw fouled off pitch after Griffith pitch, infuriating the pitcher and sparking the rule changes at the turn of the century concerning counting foul balls as strikes. Well, indeed the story may be true but I spent a good deal of time trying to document it but could not. It didn't seem to happen.

One has to realize that many of the stories we know and take for granted as fact, are often based on players or participants memories long after the fact. In this case, McGraw had the ear of New York writers for decades and fed them story after story. Many were true, many not – often the facts and specifics were jumbled or exaggerated. That's just how people are – oral history is wrought with errors and inaccuracies. They are very hard to overcome for researchers also. Who would people believe – the esteemed

McGraw or some guy years later citing some mundane or boring fact to refute the great manager?

Along these lines, McGraw rewrote history. He told stories to New York reporters about the great Baltimore Orioles' teams of the 1890s, a team that because of McGraw's efforts has a certain mythology about it. It's hard then to tell readers that the Boston club earlier in the decade was just as combative and successful, as well as others during the era. Similarly, certain works rewrite history, usually for a self-serving purpose – specifically autobiographies and the like. Albert Spalding's *America's National Game* comes to mind. One has to weed through the material to distinguish fact from, well, less factual material.

Anyway, I digress. The purpose of this book is to point beginning researchers in the right direction. Firsthand material is always preferred. Spend the time it takes – and it takes a lot – to read through old newspapers and other materials. The journey will be well worth it. Not only will you learn more about the era you're studying but you'll unearth material that will perhaps take your project in another direction – for the best. You'll also tap into material that will likely spark your next project.

I've also included a list of sources and avenues to take to firsthand information that will enhance your project. Some sources will pan out, others won't. They all need to be visited though to ensure that you've hit upon all the information that can be found at the time of your study. I've presented my view of each source and its value. Of course, that may not jive exactly with other's views but that's why we're all individuals.

Good luck and happy hunting.

By the way, learn a lesson from one of my mistakes. Instead of jumping into a major project like a book, start off with much shorter articles and hone your skills and confidence before going on to the next level.

Brian McKenna

March 2010

Chapter One

SELECTING YOUR FIELD OF STUDY

Each person has to define their own field of study; it's personal and has to be something that spurs you on. Feed your passion and let it take you in its own route, which may not be clearly defined at this point. Be open to the material, it may take you in directions which you never foresaw.

Many individuals are solely interested in only their hometown team or their favorite one. Some are more focused on individuals, often the Hall of Famers. Just realize that extensive research has been done in many cases. For example, how much new material can be presented in the 2010s about Babe Ruth? Some, surely, there are quality works to come on the Bambino - but, how about a lesser-known name? There are probably more opportunities elsewhere. Will they be as marketable, possibly, possibly not? Make it interesting and exciting and you'll gain a following.

So, how about a topic? It's always great to see new material. Something that hasn't been explored yet, or to the extent you want to present it. There are numerous opportunities here. A reinterpretation of an old story can also be a fascinating read.

Some stumble upon certain material that others haven't tapped yet. For example, your place of residence may offer some unique insight into an individual, team or other facet of baseball history. If you live in Gettysburg, Pennsylvania, could you find out more about native son Eddie Plank than someone who lives in say Des Moines, Iowa?

The point is to pick a topic that interests you. There are no limits – the history of baseball is vast. Baseball history has probably produced more articles and books that most other topics. Off the top of my head, only World War II and the Civil War can rival it. Baseball transcends both as the wars are only a small subset of possible baseball material.

Initially, pick a topic that you can easily manage. Then, work your way into deeper material that requires you to spread your wings. Think of the researching process as a journey. Small steps will eventually lead to greater accomplishments. You'll learn more about the process with each step and produce better and better works as time goes by. I look at my early work now and see how I could have improved it – as I probably will do again in a few years with what I producing now.

Zero-in on a topic and try to have some idea of the materials out there that will help you along the way – and the time that it would take to produce the work. Some works you could probably knock out in a few weeks; others may be on your back burner for years.

Learn more about your field everyday and force yourself to pull in more material each week and to put something on paper. Listen, few become rich in this endeavor. We all have other jobs. But if you don't force yourself to make headway on a regular basis, you won't. And, your efforts will just sit in some file on your desk or in a cabinet.

Chapter Two

AVAILABLE RESOURCES

There are so many avenues of resources that I'll never be able to mention them all, or even come close. More and more are being developed every day. Luckily, we live in the age of the internet and instant communication. The digital world offers opportunities that just weren't possible a decade ago and has perhaps unlimited potential. I can sit home today in Baltimore and page through the *Oshkosh Daily Northwestern* or the *Syracuse Herald*, for example, from a hundred-plus years ago.

The following is just a small listing of what's out there. Hopefully, I presented enough to get you started.

BOOKS

Books are valuable, despite the preference for firsthand material. Invaluable information – or leads to information – often hides between the covers. Many authors demand your respect and, hence, your attention. They offer great insight and present new material with each publication.

The problem is amassing a library or at least tapping into one. At some point, you're just going to have to fork over some cash for a prized publication that you just can find anywhere else. Who wouldn't want to build their library, but it's expensive? Some books can be had for pennies, other for Jacksons. I have used the following web sites to purchase materials:

Amazon.com

Barnesandnoble.com

Blackstoneaudio.com

Ebay.com

Half.com

Scholarsbookshelf.com

Since we all know how to shop, I'll concentrate on ways to read for free. Obviously, libraries are a great resource. For example, I live in Baltimore County and have access to two library systems – the county and the city. Don't just stop at the local public library; their resources tend to be limited. Hit the college libraries. They have fine collections. You don't have to be a student to sit in a corner and read their collections.

Books.google.com is great. They are adding more and more pieces all the time. Problem is not all the pages are available in most of the works. Sometimes you need to get your hands on that specific work. There is an option - "Find in a library" - while the work is on the screen that allows you to find the publication in a nearby library. Well, hopefully, it can be located nearby. For example, I pulled up *Black Baseball Entrepreneurs* by Michael E. Lomax. It tells me that I can get my hands on a copy at Johns Hopkins University (5 miles away) or at the Enoch Pratt Free Library (7 miles away).

Do not overlook works that aren't necessarily baseball in nature. Local histories, for example, can carry significant baseball material. There are numerous other non-baseball-specific works that will prove essential.

In Appendix A – Topic Bibliography - you'll find a listing of some books that are beneficial for certain topics or eras in baseball history.

JOURNALS, ARTICLES AND OTHER PUBLICATIONS

Like books, there are many sources for articles on baseball history topics. You can find many simply through Google searches. While some searches may not actually present the body of the work, they will alert you to the fact that they exist. Then, it is up to you to find a way to gain access, such as, through purchasing the material, by contacting the author or via another method.

Quite a few articles are generated by and for members of the Society for American Baseball Research and will be discussed in a separate section.

Project Muse is an online database which carries over 200 journals. For example, they carry current and past volumes of *Nine: A Journal of Baseball History and Culture* and other sports related publications. Individuals must pay fees to access the information, but you may be able to gain access to Project Muse through a local college or university library for free. I do. There are other related online databases, such as, Questia.com.

There are other journals such as the following which can be accessed through various methods, possibly with little or no cost:

- *Baseball: A Journal of the Early Game*
- *Black Ball: A Journal of the Negro Leagues*
- *Elysian Fields Quarterly: The Baseball Review*

Certain journals which may not be dedicated to baseball, or even sports, carry potentially valuable research and material for the baseball history fan.

MICROFILM

Many libraries carry microfilm of old local newspapers.

WEB SITES

Web sites will be the focus of the following chapter.

DIGITAL ARCHIVES

A listing of digital archives and methods of searching them will be explored in subsequent chapters.

FORUMS AND MESSAGE BOARDS

Computer forums and message boards will be discussed in the chapter on communication.

GOVERNMENT ENTITIES

States, counties, cities and localities have invaluable information related to individuals. Birth and death certificates are prime examples. In order to obtain the information, you'd need to directly contact the individual departments and may have to pay a small fee.

Keep in mind some material is just not available. While doing research on Eddie Plank, I kept seeing references to the fact that his birth name might have been "Stewart Edward" instead of "Edward Stewart." Unfortunately, for the era of his birth, Pennsylvania doesn't have birth certificates. Along these lines, it is difficult to pry personal information from Pennsylvania offices. This causes a problem because a great many professional ballplayers during the first half century-plus of the game hailed from PA.

Frank Russo has done a great deal of work in baseball necrology. He has gained hundreds of death certificates material. His website – Thedeadballera.com – is a valuable resource. He is working intently on prying information from Pennsylvania and other localities.

HISTORICAL SOCIETIES AND THE LIKE

Some areas have special libraries or historical societies that carry local historical information. These tend to be unique sources and often prove to be invaluable. For example, I went to the Adams County (PA) Historical Society to look for information on Eddie Plank who lived in Gettysburg. There I found some clippings of old newspaper articles. Some I had seen before but others I hadn't. I also found quite a few handwritten notes by various individuals on Plank family genealogy. What surprised me were full accounting sheets listing the dispersal of Plank's estate and trust funds that he set up for his wife and son. I wasn't really interested in them, but it made me think about the potential of stumbling upon such information and tidbits.

In another example, at the Historical Society of Washington, D.C. is a scrapbook kept by a man named Edmund F. French from the early amateur years of the game. It includes the Nationals of Washington, D.C.'s constitution from 1859 and a subsequent revision. The information proved useful in a biography I wrote on Arthur Pue Gorman.

Similar items can be found throughout the country at various locations. Visit nearby locations and you might be able to unearth something few have seen before. Keep in mind that there may be a small fee for perusing the backroom files, as well as, copying costs. You are usually expected to only use pencil while taking notes and may be required to wear gloves to preserve the material.

Many of these institutions also provide archival assistance, allowing individuals to obtain copies of materials or other assistance remotely. There will typically be hourly fees and copying and shipping costs for this help. Some places may just ask for a small donation.

BASEBALL HALL OF FAME

Naturally, the National Baseball Hall of Fame in Cooperstown, New York has a great deal of material – even outside their awe-inspiring exhibits. Collections and papers have been donated to or otherwise obtained by the museum since the mid-1930s. The library has nearly 3,000,000 items. Files are kept on most players. These files are a great starting point for any biographer. It would be a shame to overlook this valuable resource.

The individual Hall of Fame files may be small or large. As an example, while writing a biography of Clark Griffith, I obtained a copy of his Hall of Fame file. I did it remotely – by paying the librarian for his time and for copying fees. It cost around $150, but that was a large file. Smaller files would be significantly less. The Griffith file contained pictures, newspaper clippings, genealogical information and personal papers. The personal papers included copies of telegrams and other communications between Griffith and others, mainly Garry Herrmann. There were also notes Griffith made about his payroll and such on various hotel stationary. The items proved essential.

It's a hit or a miss as far as what might be in the files. Many papers have been thrown away of the years by the individuals and teams as a course of doing business, but you might stumble upon valuable communications or contracts or any number of interesting pieces.

It's best if you could spend some time at the Hall of Fame library and do some research in the files or peruse the publications. For example, if you were writing a bio of say Jimmy Dykes, you'd like to peak in his file, as well as, Connie Mack's and others. You're expected to only use pencil while taking notes and may be required to wear gloves if touching sensitive material. There will also be copying costs.

If you ask for assistance from a librarian, there will be hourly fees and copying and shipping costs for this assistance. If you wish to use a picture from their archives in a book or for a cover, there will be additional costs that would need to be negotiated.

OTHER MUSEUMS

There are other museums throughout the country that might prove useful. The Negro league Museum in Kansas City is one example. I used to work at the Babe Ruth Birthplace when it was also the Orioles museum. I can tell you for a fact that they presented good information and had an array of interesting material in the back room. They also had some special

Baltimore Colts' pieces and films. The lesson here is to stick your nose wherever you can and sniff out the rare nuggets that would fit nice in or could be the centerpiece of your writing and research.

SABR

The Society for American Baseball Research was founded in 1971 and is based in Cleveland, Ohio. According to their web site – Sabr.org:

"The purpose of SABR is to foster the research, preservation, and dissemination of the history and record of baseball. SABR shall carry out that mission through programs:

- To encourage the study of baseball, past and present, as a significant athletic and social institution;

- To encourage further research and literary efforts to establish and maintain the accurate historical record of baseball;

- To encourage the preservation of baseball research materials;

- To help disseminate educational, historical and research information about baseball."

For the year 2010, an individual membership cost $65 a year. There is a fee schedule with alternate rates for multi-year, family, under-30, senior, North American and oversees memberships.

SABR offers a wide range of advantages for members and fans. Your membership includes copies of their publications:

- The Baseball Research Journal, published twice a year
- The National Pastime, published yearly
- SABR Bulletin, published quarterly

You will also be sent other publications. In the past, that included such titles as *Deadball Stars of the American League*, *Deadball Stars of the National League* and a biography of Lefty Grove for example. They also offer free downloads of the annual *The Emerald Guide to Baseball*.

You also gain access to:

- Membership directory
- Research committees – membership and publications
- SABR lending library - microfilm archives
- SABR-L – email discussions
- SABR research exchange
- SABR online encyclopedia
- Local chapter meetings and affairs

SABR has numerous committees which produce valuable research material. For example, the Biographical Research Committee seeks to locate or update biographical information on all major leaguers – new and old. This data includes full name, birth date and location, death date and location and various other data. This information is then made available and eventually picked up by the online encyclopedias.

If you pull up a player on say Retrosheet.org and see an unknown complete name, birth or death information, you can be assured that the Biographical committee has him in their sights and are seeking information on that individual.

A lot of the biographical data that is listed at the reference sites is just plain wrong in my opinion. A good bit of it was obtained by the Hall of Fame decades ago in a survey that they mailed to players and former players' families. Many of the birth dates and locations were taken from these questionnaires. I'm of the belief that some of it is wrong. Even if 10% is wrong that's just misinformation we take for granted is a fact. The Biographical committee works to fix this.

I'll give you an example. I wrote 55 biographies for the SABR Biography Project and after doing genealogical searches, I found information that was contradictory to the encyclopedias in at least ten cases; that's nearly 20%. Some examples can be striking. I found Sandy Nava as an infant in the 1860 U.S. Census when the encyclopedias said he was born in 1850. His real name was also much different than previously identified. Clyde Day who brought fame to Pea Ridge, Arkansas wasn't actually born in Pea Ridge, or Arkansas. He was born in Center, Missouri. He grew up in Pea Ridge but still there is a distinction and a family history that was previously skewed.

I tell you about the Biographical committee because this is something happening behind the scenes at SABR that provides a great value to the baseball community. Their work isn't known but you see it every day when logging onto Baseball-reference.com or Retrosheet.org.

SABR produces other work that I use in many projects. Here is a partial list (some of these are accessible without a membership):

- The SABR Biography Project contains serious biographies on hundreds, soon-to-be thousands, of individuals associated with the game.
- David Ball's *The Nineteenth Century Transaction Register* provides insight into trades and player movements during baseball's early years.
- The College Index lists players and their colleges and vice-versa.
- The Military Index lists those that served. I particularly like the Civil War database.
- Many issues of the *Baseball Research Journal* and *The National Pastime* are online.
- The SABR Encyclopedia is expanding and includes information on scouts that isn't easily found elsewhere.

Another major reason for becoming a SABR member is the free access to an archive site, which among other newspapers provides *The Sporting News* digital archives. To tell you the truth, *TSN* is hard to read and search during certain years in its current digital form but the pages are there. It just might take some work to get to your destination.

Chapter Three

WEB SITES

There are numerous web sites that concentrate on baseball and baseball history. Other sites that may not be baseball-specific can also prove valuable. Some are popping up all the time, some wither, some are actively maintained and others are not.

There is no way to list and evaluate all of them. I'll review the ones I use regularly and some of their benefits. Later in the chapter, I'll list some sites by topic that I've found useful. However, the best way to become familiar with the sites and their benefits is to use them yourself.

BASEBALL-REFERENCE.COM

Baseball-reference.com is a site, like Retrosheet.org and Baseball-alamanc.com, that I call an encyclopedia site because it covers the statistics traditionally available in the MacMillan encyclopedia and *Total Baseball*. I mostly use the stats at Baseball-reference.com and Retrosheet.org interchangeably and at times prefer one over the other for doing varying searches.

A typically player-specific page at Baseball-reference.com carries full major league batting, fielding and pitching statistics. Biographical data is also available that lists the following information if known:

- Batting and throwing hand
- Height and weight
- Full name
- Birth date and location
- Debut and final date in the majors
- Death date and location
- Hall of Fame inclusion data is applicable
- Interment location
- List of any major league relatives
- List of attended high schools and colleges

Also from the player location one can find:

- One click relocation to home run log
- One click relocation to possible minor league teams and stats
- One click relocation to the player's individual major league teams by year
- One click relocation to the Bullpen which is a narrative biography
- List of the player's "Appearances on Leader Boards, Awards and Honors" by year and career
- One click relocation to the full yearly lists from above
- Listing of "black ink," "gray ink" and other statistical evaluators
- Listing of players with similar statistical output
- Listing of transactions information (powered by Retrosheet.org)
- Listing of known salary information
- One-click relocation to the player's yearly uniform designs

Keep in mind that school, minor league, transaction and salary information may be incomplete or inaccurate and should be verified. The Bullpen section is 'what it is.' There may be a great deal of useful information or little or none. The site will also be adding Negro League and winter Cuban League statistics in the future.

There is also a one-click function called "SCAPY" at the leader board section for individual statistics. SCAPY is an acronym:

- S = single season leaders
- C = career leaders
- A = active leaders
- P = progressive leaders
- Y = yearly leaders

From the home page of Baseball-reference.com, one can access:

- Play index
- Individual players, managers, leagues, teams
- Leader boards
- Award listings
- Postseason statistics and other detail
- Box scores (incomplete)
- Bullpen
- Minor leagues

At the minor league home page, individual players, teams, leagues, leaders, affiliates and ballparks can be accessed, as well as, various other information. Minor league information can also be found in the Bullpen.

The site includes a good deal of other data including:

- Various sections to create customized statistics and to do various other numbers-related evaluations
- All-Star Game history and statistics
- Biographical information by country, state and locality
- A blog
- Draft data
- "Baseball frivolities and fun stuff"
- Home run encyclopedia
- Oracle
- Tutorial videos

- Collegiate baseball information
- Travel guide

I prefer to use Baseball-reference.com rather than Retrosheet.org at times for a couple of reasons. One, the minor league section is a great plus. Two, I find it easier to move between players – simply type in a name and hit search.

I also use it for progressive leader boards just because that's where someone directed me at one point. I'm not a big statistic evaluator and I have no preference between the two sites for utilizing their specific numbers.

RETROSHEET.ORG

There are differences in the player pages in Retrosheet.org than Baseball-reference. For example:

- Internment information is expanded
- Managing and umpiring first and last game information is provided
- Umpiring data is provided
- Ejection information is provided
- One click relocation to the SABR Biography Project
- Fewer statistics are available in Retrosheet.org player pages

From the home page of Retrosheet.org, one can reach the following data:

- Individual player, manager, coaching and umpiring sheets
- Transaction information
- Game, year, team and league information
- Postseason and All-Star data
- Awards, Top performances, no-hitters and cycles and milestones section
- Ballpark listings and data
- Biographical information by country, state and locality

- Data downloads: Play-by-play files, game logs and schedules
- Noteworthy events, special features and research papers

I prefer Retrosheet.org over Baseball-reference.com in several instances. First, there are no ads on Retrosheet.org; thus, when I'm using a dial-up network, things run faster. Second, I prefer hoping from year to year and using their standings, roster and game log sections. Third, Retrosheet.org also seems more responsive to biographical data updates. Fourth, it also has umpiring, ejection and coaching information.

I also tend to get interment information from Retrosheet.org and prefer the transaction information. I like the "Directory of Major League Years" which offers access to (by years):

- Standings
- Individual team data
- Leader boards
- Top individual performances
- Top team performances
- Team totals
- Splits
- Players by position listing
- Umpires
- Calendar
- Team rosters (alphabetical or positional)
- Game logs
- Ballpark info

Again, I'm not a stats maven and have no opinion about which site is best along these lines. I have done only cursory statistical evaluations at both sites and am not qualified to speak on the array of statistical information that can be customized and tweak to one's specific needs. I would suggest for those who want to know this to ask at a forum for assistance. A particularly useful stat site is Tangotiger.net.

BASEBALL-ALMANAC.COM

Baseball-almanac.com is also of great assistance, providing some of the same data that can be found on the player pages at the previous two sites.

It also includes special sections on:

- All-Star Game
- Playoffs
- Autographs
- Awards
- Ballparks
- Baseball cards
- Baseball charts
- Families
- Biographies
- Book shelf
- College baseball
- Downloads
- "Fabulous Feats"
- Famous firsts
- Fun and games
- Gave sites
- Hall of Fame
- Hitting charts
- Humor and jokes
- Interviews
- "Legendary Lists"
- Managers
- Movies
- Obituaries
- Opening Day
- Pitching charts
- Poetry and songs
- Quotes
- Record books
- Rules

- Scoring
- "Statmaster"
- Stats 101
- Team by Team
- U.S. presidents
- Umpires
- World Series
- Year by Year
- Box scores
- "Today in Baseball History"

I often use Baseball-almanac.com for their timeline of rule changes and other tidbits which are nice to find listed in one place.

Baseball-almanac.com is also the source for one of the most valuable resources I know – Baseball-fever.com, a discussion forum that I for one visit daily.

GOOGLE.COM

I really don't need to tout the advantages of search engines. I'll just make a few comments. Baseball fans will also find the following helpful:

- Books.google.com
- Scholar.google.com
- News.google.com/archivesearch
- Images.google.com

Use both broad and narrow searching techniques and various approaches to each subject. For Example, these are but a few searches you can use to find information on say Sandy Nava.

- Sandy Nava
- "Sandy Nava"
- Nava
- Simental

- "Vincente Simental"
- Vincent Nava
- "Vincent Nava"
- Vincente Nava
- "Vincente Simental"
- Sandy Irwin
- "Sandy Irwin"
- Vincent Irwin
- "Vincent Irwin"

Plugging in just the player's name like this can lead to many great finds that are outside strict baseball guidelines. Most prevalent might be genealogical information. You may also find out thing about someone that you didn't know previously, such as, the fact that Arthur Irwin developed and patented a football scoreboard. Something like this may not be discovered with a baseball-specific search.

Plug in everything you can think of relating to that person – their teams, teammates, achievements, significant events and dates, etc. There is no telling what might pop up with a little creative search criterion. In the Nava example, plug in his name with additional words, such as:

- Baseball
- "Base ball"
- "San Francisco"
- Mexico
- Mexican
- "Monte Ward" or another variant of his name
- Radbourn
- Gilligan
- Providence
- Baltimore
- Oakland
- "Pacific League"
- "California League"
- Mother's name or just the word mother
- Father's name or just the word father
- Sibling name(s) or the words brother, sister

- An author's name that did research on the individual
- A book title
- Latin
- Reno
- Athletics
- Grays
- Orioles
- "Jerry Denny"
- "Jim Whitney"
- "Charlie Sweeney"
- Catcher
- Spaniard
- California
- All his managers' names
- "Union Association"
- Norfolk
- Cemetery name

With each player, it's different. Just find what works. I keep a list of search words and use them with each vehicle I use to search for a player. Sometimes, I have to go back to certain resources and plug in new search words that I found to be effective later on.

Isolate some uncommon words that can be used to search a subject easily. When I was researching black players from baseball's early era, the word "colored" helped tremendously while searching – more so in newspapers but you get the idea. The term is offensive today but was commonly bantered about in print back in the day.

The men and women associated with the game whose name is on the uncommon side are much easier to search. You can easily see how Radbourn or Nava or Gilligan would be easier to search for than Jones or Smith or Walker.

Names that are also common words in the American language or are place names are problematic and can be highly frustrating – such as – ward, joy, field, start, derby, brown, Troy, York, London, etc. A last name that is a common first name – like Henry or Thomas – will also yield many false search possibilities and waste your time; unfortunately, it's unavoidable.

WIKIPEDIA.ORG

The knock is never to trust Wikipedia. But, I don't find that to be the case. Like all information you get, you need to verify it. Wikipedia is great at providing good information and leading you to sources and giving you further leads on a topic. Just verify your data.

AGATE TYPE

Gary Ashwill has a blog – Agatetype.typepad.com – which is definitely worth checking out. He has unique items of great interest and is always on the prowl to dig up something yet seen.

BASEBALLHISTORYBLOG.COM

My site – titled "Glimpses in Baseball History" - which is just at its genesis at the writing of this material. It highlights tidbits from baseball history which aren't common knowledge or generally discussed.

SITES BY TOPIC

EARLY BASEBALL

19cbaseball.com
Baseballchronology.com

BIOGRAPHY

Marquiswhoswho.com
Bioproj.sabr.org

Baseballlibrary.com (I like their Chronology section)

Bioguide.congress.gov/biosearch/biosearch.asp

Distinguishedwomen.com

Makeithappen.com/wis

Blogofdeath.com

MINOR LEAGUES

Minorleagueresearcher.blogspot.com

Minorleaguebaseball.com

Espn.com

Baseball-reference.com

Thebaseballcube.com

BLACK BASEBALL

Agatetype.typepad.com

Negroleaguebaseball.com

Nlbpa.com

Nlbm.com

Blackbaseball.com

Thediamondangle.com

Baseball-statistics.com/negro-lg/#bio

INTERNATIONAL BASEBALL

Japanesebaseball.com

Baseballguru.com

Thediamondangle.com

Japanball.com

Agatetype.typepad.com

Japanbaseballdaily.com

The Japan Times online

Cubanball.com

Bjarkman.com

Fordham University library site

Latinobaseball.com

Japanese Baseball Hall of Fame site

Robsjapanesecards.com

Latinosportslegends.com

Salondelafama.com.mx

Canadian baseball hall of fame site

Canadian sports hall of fame site

BUSINESS OF BASEBALL

Roadsidephotos.sabr.org/baseball/bbblog.htm

MISCELLANEOUS

Digitalgallery.nypl.org

Baseballthinkfactory.org

Findagrave.com

Thedeadballera.com

Baseballinwartime.com

Hisotricbaseball.com

Agatetype.typepad.com

Basealllibrary.com

Mlb.com

Espn.com

Si.com

The Library of Congress site (Spalding books and other materials)

Youtube.com (old and new footage)

Petermorrisbooks.com

National Baseball Hall of Fame site

Baseball-almanac.com

Majorleagueumpires.com

Maurybrown.com

Uniform database at Hall of Fame site

Chapter Four

DIGITAL ARCHIVES

Old newspapers and other archives will be essential to your work. Searching them will take up the bulk of your time, but the time and effort will pay off. Your work will be factual, fresh and hopefully entertaining. You'll open many eyes with all the goodies you've unearthed.

There are basically three ways to read old newspapers: physically; on microfilm; digitally. You can find microfilm and physical materials from a variety of sources:

- Public libraries
- Private libraries
- Interlibrary loan
- Historical societies and the like
- SABR Lending Library
- National Baseball Hall of Fame
- Outright purchase

It's just a matter of hunting for what you need. There may be fees and considerable wait if you request microfilm from sources outside your home base. Typically, you would visit a local library, hop on a microfilm machine and spend the day searching through material. There will be fees for copying.

The bulk of this chapter is dedicated to finding digital materials and tips for searching them. There are many sources for accessing digital databases. Many, but not all, involve paying user fees.

Run a Google search and you will find sites that offer memberships for digital databases, such as, Paperofrecord.com, Worldvitalrecords.com, Ancestry.com (and other genealogy sites), Newspaper ARCHIVE, ProQuest and others. Pay these fees and you're searching in no time. The more you pay the greater access you'll have.

Some newspaper archives are provided digitally individually (not part of a national database package) for a fee. Others concentrate on an area, such as packages of newspapers based in one county or state.

If you're like me, you'd rather do it on a limited budget. That'll be my concentration.

SABR

SABR (with a membership) offers access to Worldvitalrecords.com which includes a wide range of newspapers including *The Sporting News* and various genealogical materials. The current digital *TSN* is harder to search and read the further you go back in time but the info is there for the diligent seeker.

PUBLIC LIBRARIES

Your local public library probably offers some searchable digital databases. They're free and most can probably be accessed at home as well. As far as older papers go, my county and city libraries offer the following for free access. I can use them from home 24/7.

- *Baltimore Sun*, 1837-on
- *Baltimore Afro American*, 1893-1988
- *Christian Science Monitor*, 1908-1996
- *New York Times*, 1851-on
- *Wall Street Journal*, 1889-on
- *Washington Post*, 1877-on
- *Chicago Tribune*, 1849-on
- *Chicago Defender*, 1905-on

I only listed the above as an example as your library system(s) is likely to carry a differing assortment.

OTHER FREE DATABASES

There are quite a few other databases which can be accessed via the web for no cost:

- La84foundation.org which includes *Sporting Life* (many years 1885-1917), *Outing* (1883-1915), *Baseball Magazine* (1908-1920). There are also other non-baseball specific periodicals which deserve a glance or two.
- *Brooklyn Eagle* online archive, 1841-1902
- *Spalding   Guides*   (some   issues)   at Memory.loc.gov/ammem/collections/spalding
- *Baseball Digest* via Google
- Ancestry.com gives access to newspapers.
- Wikipedia.org – go to the site and type 'List of online newspaper archives.' A list will pop up which you can explore. Some will be fee-based.
- Baseball historian Peter Morris maintains a list of databases at his site, Petermorrisbooks.com. Some have fees, some don't
- News.google.com/archivesearch
- Various others are out there like college newspapers. You just need to go looking. I found great information on Eddie Plank at the   Gettysburg   College   newspaper   archive, Thegettysburgian.com. *The Silent Worker*, the school newspaper for the New Jersey School for the Deaf, proved an invaluable source for a piece I wrote on Reuben Stephenson.

MID-CONTINENT PUBLIC LIBRARY

The bulk of my time is spent searching the digital archives at the Mid-Continent Public Library based in Independence, Missouri. Their service is great and I highly recommend it. In fact, if you're serious about this endeavor, this source is a must.

It costs $20 a year but it's the best $20 you'll ever spend. You'll need to purchase a "Fee Paid Library Card" unless you happen to live in Independence. It's done through the genealogy section of the library at the following email address: ge@mcpl.lib.mo.us

You'll have remote access 24/7 to hundreds of newspapers. The three main sections I use are:

- **Newspaper ARCHIVE** – "Access Newspaper ARCHIVE contains tens of millions of searchable pages from over 400 cities and towns from hundreds of newspapers dating back as far as the 1700s. The collection includes coverage from the U.S., Canada, and the U.K."
- **Historical Newspapers** – "Historical Newspapers includes the following: New York Times 1851-2005, Wall Street Journal 1889-1990, Washington Post 1877-1991, Christian Science Monitor 1908-1994, Los Angeles Times 1881-1986, Chicago Tribune 1849-1986, Chicago Defender 1910-1975, Hartford Courant 1764-1984, Atlanta Daily World 1931-2003, Boston Globe 1872-1924, Los Angeles Sentinel 1934-2005, New York Amsterdam News 1922-1993, and the Pittsburg Courier 1911-2002."
- **Nineteenth Century Newspapers** – "This historical resource includes digital facsimile images of both full pages and clipped articles for hundreds of 19th century U.S. newspapers. For each issue, the newspaper is captured from cover-to-cover, providing access to every article, advertisement and illustration."

GENEALOGY

If your work is going to include biographical or genealogical material, you'll need to learn the ins and outs of the databases.

Ancestry.com is a preferred source. Many library systems provide free access to it but you usually have to do your research at the library itself. Individuals can purchase access to the site if they prefer working remotely.

Besides providing access to U.S. Census from 1930 and before, Ancestry.com also includes other resources that baseball researchers may find helpful:

- Foreign censuses
- Military service records
- Immigration records
- Ship passenger records
- Court, land, will and financial records
- Stories and publications
- Photos and maps
- Birth, marriage and death records
- Family history collections
- Voter lists
- City directories
- Burial records
- Various reference material
- Message boards and forums
- School yearbook information
- Etc.

HeritageQuest.com also provides access to U.S. Census records. My library provides this site and I can use it remotely. It provides a great deal of other information which I'm not personally familiar with but it appears that it would be helpful to many.

I also use Familysearch.com which provides a good deal of data. I usually search from the home page which leads to genealogical information that has been inputted by others. I have found many families of professional baseball players listed. The information has provided me with leads to other information, as well.

There are numerous other genealogical sites on the web. Their message boards can be extremely helpful as they will lead you to experienced researchers as well as possible living family members of the subject of your research.

SUMMARY

There are many resources which can put you on your way to unearthing valuable and exciting baseball history research. Many are free. For around $100 - the cost of this book, Mid-Continent Library access and SABR membership - you can put yourself in a much better position for success. Ultimately, your drive for baseball history research will prove to be your most valuable tool.

Chapter Five

SEARCHING RESOURCES, SITES AND ARCHIVES

Locating resources, sites and archives is just the beginning. You'll need a plan for pulling the information you need and an eye for noticing the things that you weren't expecting. The process will involve a lot of visual scanning, followed by intense reading and taking notes and citations. First, though, you'll need some techniques for approaching the varying sources at your disposal.

BOOK, JOURNALS AND ARTICLES

Publications – books and articles for the most part - are easy; we grew up with them. We know that books and articles of length are typically broken down into smaller topics to help keep things organized and maintain the interest of the reader. Don't miss some finer points as you're scanning the material for your nuggets.

The content page and index are your guides. Study each and approach the book as a collection of pieces. Research typically doesn't involve reading a whole book – that's for your leisure time. Look at the contents to decide where your focus may lie. Read the entire index. Don't just pick up a book, look at the index for your specific topic, jot those page numbers down, read them, take notes and then move on.

Other parts of the book may prove valuable as well. For example, if you're researching Ban Johnson, you may also be discussing quite a few others in your work, like Charles Comiskey, Clark Griffith, John Brush, Garry Herrmann and Judge Landis, not to mention events, conflicts and other incidents in baseball history. Note through the index what material this book covers and its methods. You'll need to know this for your next project as well. You may find yourself remembering something from that book – perhaps years later – that you'll want to draw on.

Also, note the author and his or her body of work and expertise. Check out the bibliography and especially the notes. Great insight is gained from the notes. They also contain source listings you may want to check out.

LIBRARIES, SOCIETIES, MUSEUMS, ETC.

Learn about all sources and avenues for information and how they may benefit you today and in the future.

WEB SITES

Web sites are fluid, changing every day. Keep a list of the ones you find useful. Enter them into your "Favorites." Consult the list with every project and at least mentally visit those sites to see if there is something worthwhile that can be extracted.

Get to know each site for its value and especially for its credibility. Avoid the sites that merely cut and paste from others and offer questionable data. Verify everything and trust only your tried and true resources.

RESEARCHING TIPS

Researching is not linear, you need to approach a topic from several differ angles to wring out the value of any given source. Here are some ideas which may prove useful. (I'll approach some topics from the point of view of writing and researching a biography but the same concepts apply to a topic piece.)

- Statistics can be interesting but they are more so when presented in a new way or from a new perspective. If a player had a good stretch, say three or four years, crunch some numbers and calculate some stats that others haven't. For example, calculate a multi-year ERA or OPS or slugging percentage. Or, calculate a multi-year win-loss record or strikeout-to-walk ratio. The possibilities are endless. It will be more interesting than merely relaying numbers from his career record.
- If analyzing a specific season, it would be interesting to breakdown the timeframes – often by months – for various factors. For example, when did the pitcher accrue the bulk of his wins, how many times did he strikeout 8+ or how did he perform during the pennant run from August to October? Hoss Radbourn's 1884 season can be broken down in any number of interesting ways that will keep the reader captivated, or at least not bored with a simple rehashing of numbers they can get from an encyclopedia.
- Present a player's stats in relation to contemporaries
- Present league-based stats such as ERA+ which denote a pitcher's ERA in relation to the league average
- Use the Game Log section of Retrosheet.org to break down events, stats, wins and losses or any number of nuances on a day by day, week by week or month by month basis
- Note standings and games behind – a team may be in fourth place one year but only seven games behind. That season would look quite different than one in which the second place team was 15 games behind.
- Use the Game Log section of Retrosheet.org to track daily standings. If a team finished the year three games out, was it in first place late in the season? Similarly, when did a pennant winner take the lead – did it flip flop or were they in command a month out, two months out?
- Note a teams' manager or captain, its front office management
- If you're writing about a catcher, how many games did he work in relation to teammates? To other league catchers?

- If you're writing about a pitcher, how many games did he work - and his success - in relation to teammates or other league pitchers?
- If you're writing about a pitcher, give a good indication of his repertoire and how he approached his job. Everyone wants to know this. Roger Clemens with his dominating fastball approached hitters much different than Greg Maddux did. What kind of pitches did they throw, from what angles, etc.? What was their thought process? How did they work the batter?
- How did a specific player perform before and after a rule change? For example, who fared well and who didn't when the pitching distance was lengthened to 60'6" in 1893?
- Don't fall into the belief that only the championship clubs are worth studying. The game's history is interesting no matter the final outcome of the standings.
- Track player movement between teams, especially in the minors. In baseball's early years, minor leagues and individual teams were constantly falling and rising. If one player played for say Lynn and Manchester in one season in the New England League (or even jumping to another league), find out what happened. Did Lynn fold? Did he transfer with one or more teammates? You'll find nuances like in 1892 the entire Tacoma team of the Pacific Northwest League went en masse to Missoula, Montana after the PNL folded.
- Did one player follow a certain manager from team to team, especially in the minors? You'll find this was prevalent, especially in the nineteenth century.
- Note interesting teammates a player may have had. For example, one of Clark Griffith's minor league teammates was Pacer Smith who had an interesting history himself. Smith's story could add some spice to a Griffith bio.
- Certain individuals will tend to crop up in another ballplayer's career. Describe and document their relationship.
- Expect and even welcome that your current project might lead to your next project. I wrote a bio of Eddie Plank which led me to a subsequent project, the Bethlehem Steel League. I wrote one bio on a deaf ballplayer and before I was finished, I had four different pieces written on different deaf players. Often, the information overlaps so each subsequent project becomes a little easier. The sources often overlap, which can speed up researching.

- I've picked projects just because I didn't know anything about them or had even heard of the subject. A project on Arthur Pue Gorman led me to research the Ellipse ball field on the grounds of the White House.

- One of the biggest mistakes one can make about the past is to judge it from today's standards. I try, but am not always successful, to present things nonjudgmental in my writings. Sure, it's easy to criticize Cap Anson for his stand against black players but he was just one guy; everyone else was right there with him. In economics, they have terms for presenting and evaluating issues in this fashion. First, there is normative economics. As the name implies, normative values are used to evaluate something, say X. Second, in positive economics, X is merely presented how it is. There are no political or moral judgments tied to its worth. 'It is what it is' in modern vernacular. The point of view that you decide to tell you story can have a great affect on or to your reader, sometimes for the better, sometimes not.

- Naturally, things were done differently in the past; understand to what extent. An example here is college baseball. In the nineteenth and early twentieth centuries, there were different operational procedures, eligibilities and the like. Many colleges had preparatory departments, essentially high schools, attached to them. You can call up Eddie Plank on one of the reference sites and see that he went to Gettysburg College. In fact, he was enrolled in the preparatory department. He did play on the main college nine but he never attended the college proper.

- Sometimes coming to the root of why a ballplayer changed his name or how he gained a nickname can be an interesting story in and of itself.

- Don't assume that because a ballplayer had a lengthy minor league career and a short or nonexistent major league one meant that he was an inferior ballplayer. Obviously, that isn't the case with many black players but others as well. For example, why didn't Frank Shellenback stay in the majors?

- I like to avoid common descriptions, terms or ideas that others use over and over. While researching Bud Fowler, I noticed that nearly every piece on him included the word 'itinerant.' It made it seem like everyone was just copying and pasting from each other. Consequently, I wrote a twenty page bio on him without using the word once.

NEWSPAPER ARCHIVES

Researching old newspaper archives can be tedious, boring and time consuming. But, the rewards are many. When doing so digitally, you'll need to certain keep things in mind. Obviously, old newspapers are being scanned onto a computer and then the computer reads them. Errors can and will happen during the scanning process. The slightest imperfection and the computer might read a "U" as an "I" or an "O." I'd imagine that the variations here are endless.

With that in mind, a computer may read the name "Bonetti" as "Banetti," "Bonatti" or a number of similarities – you get the idea. You'd need to search for them. Also, don't assume that there was a common spelling for a ballplayer's name back in the day. Different writers used Radbourn or Radbourne or Radburne or the like. Just tinker with the name Delahanty and see what pops up. Also with Radbourn as an example, you'll have to check different first names or nicknames, such as, Charles, Charlie, Charley, Old Hoss or anything else you might come across.

AN EXAMPLE AND MORE RESEARCH TIPS

Here's how I might approach researching a biography using Eddie Plank as an example, a piece I completed recently.

First, I'll look at his name and ponder what challenges it might hold. The word "plank" is in the dictionary but it's not common enough to cause a great deal of trouble – some yes, but I'm reasonably happy with it. There doesn't seem to be too many variations of the name, so it'll be pretty clean researching him. (This won't always be the case, especially the farther you go back in time.)

Okay, so where do I start? I print up a fresh 'Resource Checklist' like the one I included in Appendix B. I'll need to consider every possible source and check them off as I do.

Next, I'll read a general, not too in depth, biography of Mr. Plank so I have a general idea of the man and the different eras in his life. Works that provide short biographies include *Baseball's First Stars, Nineteenth Century Stars*, biographical encyclopedias or any number of web sites. I'll check out Baseball-reference.com to note what years I'll be searching and to get an idea of his minor league career.

I like to first delve into a player's life by examining his time before and after his baseball career or his life outside the game, so to speak. There will be much less data immediately available in these areas. Can I paint a full picture of this man's life? - Sometimes yes, sometimes no. After sorting through my available material on his time outside the game and Googling it on the web to a good extent, I hit the archives – genealogy sites and old newspapers. In truth, I may just jump right into Ancestry.com before all else and find his family.

An initial search at Ancestry.com might pull up the man at various Censuses or other documents during the course of his life. I start there. There are a couple things to keep in mind here:

- Currently, Censuses are only available through 1930.
- Much of the 1890 Census was destroyed in a fire.
- The 1900 Census is the only one that lists month and year of birth.
- Early 19th century Censuses only include the head of household's name and tick marks for other household members.
- The 1880 Census is the only one that can be searched by occupation. As an exercise, plug "baseball," "base," "ball" or "player" into that Census and see what pops up.
- The World War I Civilian Draft Registration carries a wide array of information for men born between 9/11/1872 and 9/12/1900, such as, full name, date and place of birth, place of residence, occupation and employer. The WWII database carries similar data.
- It is possible to find individuals and their families in foreign censuses. I have done so in the Canadian Census.

Ideally, the major documents will pop up on an initial search. Here are some things you'd like to see.

- All Censuses throughout his lifetime
- Military documents
- Passport applications
- Ship passenger listings
- Other immigration documents
- Social Security Death Index
- Birth, marriage and death records
- U.S. Obituary Collection
- City directory listings

Not all of these will pop up; you'll have to go looking for them. Search far and wide and use any parameter you can think of to land that valued document. For example, if I was looking for Edward Plank but couldn't find him in a certain Census, I'd use what I could. If he had a sister or wife named say Josephine, it might help. Josephine isn't as common as Edward.

The following factors can be inputted or not in your effort to help widen or narrow the search:

- First and/or last name
- State, county and/or township
- Birthplace
- Estimated birth year
- Immigration year
- Marital status
- Gender
- Race
- Relation to head of household
- Father's given name and/or birthplace
- Mother's given name and/or birthplace
- Spouse's given name
- Occupation

The problem may rest with the surname. If it was illegible or sloppily written, Ancestry.com might have Plank listed any number of ways. Sometimes you'll find it by luck, other times not at all. You could always just do a page by page search of where you believe he may have lived but that's a hit or miss, and time consuming. Sometimes, there is no other way.

Search as best as you can and set a time limit for your seeking. Some data just isn't worth the time it'll take to find it. You may never find certain documents. Just remember the missing data and hope you come across some items in the newspapers. There, you'll occasionally find marriage announcements, death and/or illness of family members or any array of information. *The Sporting News* and *Sporting Life* paid a good bit of attention to players' personal lives, as did hometown newspapers. Again, it's a hit or a miss.

Some individuals may be listed multiple times in a certain year. Since the Census is taken throughout the year, you may find Plank living with his family in Gettysburg in January and again with teammates in Philadelphia or another town in June.

I can't give you all the possible scenarios you'll run into; there are too many. Just hop on, try it out, make mistakes and learn from it all.

In Plank's lifetime, 1875-1926, you'd want to pull up the 1880, 1900, 1910 and 1920 Censuses. It may also be beneficial for your project to locate his parents, siblings, spouse(s) or children in the 1860, 1870 or 1930 Censuses.

The Censuses can tell you a wide array of things, some of which may be common knowledge, some of which may debunk common knowledge:

- Location of family
- His name – not always straight forward. You'll find many variations; some men went by their middle name, some went by different names throughout their lifetime.
- Parents and siblings' names
- Birthplaces and dates of the subject and his or her parents, siblings, spouse(s) and children. This may help identify family movements. If siblings or children were born in different locations, the family was moving about.

- Grandparents and other family members can also be found – some will live close by, always check for similar names or for in-laws
- Immigration dates
- Naturalization dates
- The 1900 Census lists how many children a woman had and how many were alive at the time.
- Occupations
- English reading and writing capabilities
- Marriage timeframes
- Spouse and children's names and data
- Birthplace(s) of an individual's parents
- Street addresses
- Whether they rent or own a home
- Live-in servants or boarders
- Net worth
- Property values or expenditures
- Date the Census was taken
- Sex and race of individuals
- Medical infirmities
- Listing of neighbors
- Much more
- The Canadian Census was quite intrusive and may have data related to hours worked per week, salary and even religious affiliation.

Also, the absence of people in a given Census will tell you things, such as the possible death of a family member. Other documents will provide similar data and help you fill in the blanks of your subject's life.

Keep in mind that Census records are not the end all. Age listings and other data may vary slightly or greatly from one Census to the next. When you weigh all the information obtained, things may not add up. Your research may just be a starting point. Locate birth, marriage and death certificates and the like for firmer information.

I'll check other genealogy sites for Plank and his family and run Google.com and Books.google.com searches for similar information. All the while, I'll be scooping up other data, probably baseball related - for future examination - that happens to cross my path.

Next, I'll hit the newspapers for Plank from 1874 to 1900 and from 1918 to 1926, his time on Earth outside the majors and/or minors. A likely place to start is the Gettysburg newspapers, as he lived his entire life there. Other subjects may have moved around substantially and will have to be tracked down.

I'll start with searches for "Eddie Plank" and "Edward Plank" limited by location for each time period. Then, I branch out to include all locations. This may give some good hits. Realize that the further you go back in time players were typically just known by their last names.

At some point, the search will need to be broadened, which will generate more hits. Thus, certain searches may require limitations to location and time period. I'll search for the words Plank plus:

- His hometown
- His schools
- His amateur clubs
- His semi-pro clubs
- His time at Gettysburg College
- His jobs outside the game
- Early baseball career
- Baseball after his active career – possibly umpiring, managing, coaching or executive work, etc.
- I'll want to locate any obituaries or other articles that might discuss his medical problems or possibly his funeral or other events
- Any number of words or terms I might come across to help pull out the nuggets

I'll also run searches for his parents, siblings, wife, children, etc. Certain facets of Plank's life may require independent searches. For example, I'll want to know more about the following even if his name is not mentioned:

- His schools
- His amateur clubs
- His semi-pro clubs
- Teammates
- Etc.

It's also a good idea to check sources well after his death. Quite a bit could be found. Even before he was born, there might be articles on his parents or grandparents.

After I've thoroughly investigated the years 1876-1900 and 1918 to 1926, it's time for the baseball years. The hits will probably be numerous so each database will have to be searched a year at a time, sometimes a day, week or month at a time if something out of the ordinary occurred that would generate a great number of hits.

Research each event thoroughly. For important dates, pull up box scores and make sure the information corresponds to your other research. Read the game recaps for further information.

Now's the time to use Appendix C to document the player's time during each year that he may have changed teams, or been injured, suspended or otherwise absent.

At all times, be on the lookout for items you can quote, or actual quotes from or about Plank by baseball men or associates or family members, etc. These will enhance and strengthen your final product immensely. They may say things perhaps better than you can. They also expose readers to the vernacular of the era, present the climate of the time and other nuances.

Use any new-found data to augment your search parameters or to return to previously read resources for further searching.

You'll have to repeat your searches for each database you're using. For example, using the Mid-Continent Library databases, you'd have three completely separate searching phases. I usually check the Historical

Newspaper section first. It contains the major newspapers and will give you a pretty good idea of what's out there on your subject – at least the major points. It's also a bit easier to use as the articles tend to be smaller and thus easier to pull up and quicker for you to read.

Your search hits are listed for you in chronological order. Unfortunately, your search criteria are not highlighted within the text so it can be frustrating at times trying to locate your nugget if it's contained in a large article. The *Boston Globe* and *Chicago Tribune* tend to have longer baseball articles to weed through. The pages of the *New York Times* and *Washington Post* are more chopped up, so the articles tend to be shorter and more single-minded.

Second, I check the Nineteenth Century Newspapers. The search hits are listed in chronological order but the articles tend to be longer. Fortunately, it uses highlights so it's extremely quick and easy to read the pertinent information and move on to the next hit.

Finally, I check Newspaper ARCHIVE. I do this last because it takes the longest to use. The criteria are often not highlighted and hits are not presented chronologically within the timeframe you select. Also, you are presented with full pages, not cut articles; however, there is a search function which usually makes things much easier. It also presents an excerpt with each hit; thus, it's relatively easy to scan to see if this is something you're interested in.

The fact that full pages are searched tends to increase the upload time. However, this source if invaluable and will prove beneficial for the ardent seeker. It contains articles from smaller city and town newspapers. For example, it proved its worth to me while searching for Eddie Plank because Newspaper ARCHIVE carries three different Gettysburg, Pennsylvania newspapers – a big help. You're likely to gain insight and more personalized articles that the larger newspapers simply don't carry.

Another reason I check Newspaper ARCHIVE last is because of the repetition. I've already read Historical Newspapers and Nineteenth Century Newspapers, so I have a base of knowledge. Newspaper ARCHIVE is slower, so when I see repeated information, I can merely skip it.

Another thing to keep in mind with Newspaper ARCHIVE is the wire reports. Since we're dealing with a great many newspapers, there is overlap. Wire reports will be picked up and repeated throughout the country, sometimes with a significant time lag. Recognizing them quickly will allow you to move on and progress through what very well might be an extensive hit list.

Also, notice the location of the hits. You may be able to ignore many of the hits this way. If you're searching for a relatively common name or other parameter for a guy that lives in Pennsylvania, in all likelihood you can ignore the hits in say Utah with a subject by the same name. Each database can further be searched by location and even by specific newspaper if need be.

Each of these three databases operates a little differently. You'll become more proficient with each new search. As always with digital databases, limit your searches with quotes and a set timeframe or location to better manage the total number of potential hits. Also, if you're looking for something very specific narrow the timeframe and search day by day or week by week if necessary. As far as location goes, you can start with a specific newspaper, and then broaden your search to a city, state and/or country.

Similarly, the other databases you use will have their idiosyncrasies. There are tricks to searching each to make things go smoother and quicker. For example, if you wanted to search the *Sporting Life* for say Clark Griffith, try it this way:

- Type Clark Griffith with no other restrictions. This will lead to a list topped by articles that contain the phrase Clark Griffith. It will then lead into others that include Clark and Griffith.
- Then, limit the search to just Griffith and go year by year; hopefully, the hit list will be manageable. There is a short excerpt presented with each, so that helps.

Databases such as the *Brooklyn Eagle* and the Northern New York Library Network (News.nnyln.org) use other software that you'll have to adapt to.

Chapter Six

MAKING CONTACTS

No matter how much data you've accrued at this point, there is always room for more. It's time to start asking others for help. Actually, you should have already been doing this. While another may not know the entire subject as you do, he or she may have great insight into smaller areas of your project. It's also a good idea to find out who is doing similar research and the focus of their project.

FORUMS

Let's face it; our individual point of view is not always correct. It pays to scan the baseball community and take its temperature on a subject to possibly smooth out your thinking process or to adjust your approach in some manner or completely.

Discussion forums can offer a great deal of assistance. I personally visit Baseball-fever.com on a daily basis. I follow many of the discussions and add comments as I desire. I can also start threads which spark a discussion on a topic of interest to me at that time.

The forum also has an archive so that old discussions can be read or used for a reference. They will not be kept forever, so download ones of interest to you.

A forum has the potential to:

- Answer a specific question you have
- Introduce you to new ideas
- Hash through the specifics of a topic
- Present raw information
- Offer avenues to find new information
- Introduce yourself to fellow enthusiasts
- Develop a relationship with fellow enthusiasts

As a collective, the men and women who peruse and participate at a forum have a much broader base of knowledge and interest than an individual. Hence, the range of topics and point of views is immense and far-reaching. You'll be exposed to much more than you bring to the table.

Develop contacts through the forum. You are permitted to send private messages which can lead to opportunities to further your research and resource base.

A caveat though – you should enter the forum with integrity and temperance, as in all interactions. Abide by normal social customs. It is easy to get carried away with your temper and attitude when sitting in front of a keyboard as opposed to communicating one-on-one with another individual who's sitting in front of you. Show respect and it will be returned. Forums ban users everyday for their inability to assimilate positively.

There are forums out there on most any topic. It might prove useful for a baseball researcher to belong to several baseball forums, other sport forums and a general history forum to name just a few.

VARIOUS CONTACTS

At various times, it will be necessary to establish one-on-one contacts through email, snail mail, telephone or face-to-face. These contacts will prove vital.

- Librarians offer a wide range of services and knowledge. They can provide valuable information and point you towards new avenues of research or sources. Some librarians will go out of their way to help your cause. Don't limit yourself locally. I contacted a librarian in Williamstown, Massachusetts while researching Frank Grant. I wanted to know where an African-American would attend school in the area in the 1870s and 1880s. Librarians can also assist with interlibrary loans whereby you could obtain material from across the country.
- Local historians could have also helped with my Grant question. They will provide you with more information than you could ask for or know to ask for.
- General historians can help with an array of topics.
- College archivists can help you navigate and find data within their domain.
- Authors are always a great resource. The problem may be getting to them, finding their email address for example. Many belong to SABR and list their contact information in the membership directory. Some are university professors and can be located through that avenue. Some belong to forums and thus can be found. After doing my research for Old Hoss Radbourn, I was weighing a few ideas in my head. Some were new ideas on the subject and I wanted to know if I was on track. So I contacted Edward Achorn who had a book, *Fifty-Nine in '84*, on the pitcher in the works. We bantered about some ideas and I felt more comfortable with my approach. Every bit helps. Some authors can be more than gracious. They will enter prolonged discussions with you, provided sources and notes and help you gain access to their work. One even sent me several articles that he wrote and another sent me his full genealogical workup on an individual.
- Naturally, your subject or those that know or knew him or her may still be alive and receptive to a personal interview. Be prepared and knowledgeable on the subject and this will help the flow of the conversation.

- Fellow researchers, historians and baseball enthusiasts will be more interested to help you than most. Develop a network of contacts and friends within the baseball community. If I have a question about baseball in St. Louis in the nineteenth century, I know who to contact to get a good push in the right direction. If I need minor league stats of one player, I know who to contact. There are endless possibilities here.

GENEALOGICAL CONTACTS

Unless you're a genealogist entering the field of baseball research, you're going to need help. Most of us are just novices trying to make sense of a vast– and often contradictory – pool of information. You could pay a genealogist to do your search for you, but that might be expensive and prohibitive. The onus then falls back on you.

Obviously, do the best you can with the genealogical sites and materials discussed in the previous chapters. Then, branch out and get assistance. At some point, you may need to directly contact:

- The subject
- Family members
- Friends
- Neighbors
- Local historians
- Librarians
- Colleges and Universities
- Genealogist
- Government entities
- Prisons
- Churches
- Cemeteries
- Any number of potential sources

Families, schools, government entities, prison systems, churches, cemeteries and the like keep an array of records. Whether they are willing to share them with you is another question. Use your charm, persuasion, integrity, enthusiasm, intensity, temperance – whatever works.

Search and utilize genealogy message boards and blogs. Not only can you learn more about doing this type of research but they can assist in your specific quest. You may find others that are seeking information on your target or his family. These may be relatives of your subject who can further help you.

COMMON COURTESY

Build an array of contacts through goodwill. Always offer to exchange information and assistance when someone approaches you. Answer your emails promptly and others are likely to do the same.

Always divulge the root of your interest – baseball research. People will be leery of your intentions, especially if you're requesting personal information. They may be quite helpful though when you mention baseball, your project, affiliations or otherwise get them excited to assist you.

Present yourself well with everyone you contact and you'll increase your odds of getting a favorable response. Also, be aware that not everyone will be receptive to your inquiries and that some interactions may take a while to develop.

I've found that most people are receptive to inquiries concerning baseball and baseball players. Some emails that I send off go unanswered and are thus frustrating. However, I invariably hear from that individual weeks or months later when they're cleaning out their junk mail. Many emails never reach the intended inbox. Also, note the time of year. You may have a much harder time getting a response from a professor in the summer than during the spring or fall semester.

Chapter Seven

ORGANIZING YOUR DATA

As you're pulling in information, you'll have to organize it in some fashion. Here are some ideas which might prove useful.

- Keep your work in one place, nice and organized. After you've collected the data, you'll have numerous pages of information. You'll have individual pages and packets of similar information, probably stapled or held together with a binder clip. You may also have documents saved electronically.
- Keep similar information together in a packet. For example, all your genealogy information should be together in a packet for easy access. Sure, at some point you'll be reading each piece of information and setting it aside but you'll also want to quickly return to it at some point. Having all the genealogy information together hastens the process.
- Always get full citations of the sources you're pulling information from. For example, if you're writing notes from a book or article write the full citation at the top of the page and note page numbers as you're making your way through the work. It's probably best to use separate pages for each source. For a Census listing, for example, be sure to get the information you'll need to find it again such as year, state, county, city, district or ward

number, page number or roll, series and page number. Also, note the spelling of the family name that Ancestry.com or another database has the listing stored under, if it differs from your spelling. For instance, "McKenna" in the 1880 Census may be read as "Mikena" by Ancestry.com.

- Make copies of what you can –either hard or electronic copies. It'll speed up the initial researching process and give you a permanent copy. Make sure to copy any related endnotes that may be located in another part of the text.

- Repeatedly back-up your electronic data. Anything can happen. Maintain several flash drives to store your backup files and keep them stored in separate locations.

- Print and/or download digital genealogy records if you can.

- Print and/or download large newspaper articles if a good bit of the information proves useful.

- Consult the Print Preview often, especially in certain software like the one used for the *Brooklyn Eagle*. The piece of the article you want may only be on Printed Page 3. You'll save some coins just printing the page or pages that you want.

KEEPING RESOURCES HANDY

You may want to keep certain information on the side, ready for use. Whether they are hard copies or a soft copy, MS Word document for instance, is up to you. Some examples include:

- I like to keep a perpetual calendar list handy. Your research will produce dates or newspaper citations listed by day of the week, so you'll need to find those specific dates.

- Keep your contact information close. You never know when you'll have to send off an email. Users at forums are often identified by a nickname. Keep a list of their actual name if you have it so you can personalize communications.

- I carry a single flash drive with me most places that contains a great deal of information, most of my files. I can pull up what I need when I need it.

- In the travel bag that I use for research, I have an inexpensive blank flash drive just in case I leave my main one at home and need to store something.

- It does concern me that I carry one flash drive around with a lot of information. I have lost them before. Now, I attach a long, bright dog leash to the drive. It may look a little silly but it's nearly impossible for me to leave the flash drive stuck in some random computer and lost.
- Some have commented to me that they have broken one or several flash drives and, thus, lost access to their information. That's never happened to me but I don't attach the drive to my keys. Keys by nature get banged up and tossed around.
- I keep several computer files which help me while working on projects. For one, I keep a blank MS Word document. I tend to work on quite a few different computers, at libraries and elsewhere. By having a blank MS Word document, I work in the version I prefer.
- I have a Word file titled Master Bibliography. It contains all the bibliographies I typed in on previous projects. Since I invariably use some sources over and over again, I can copy and paste from the Master Bibliography into my current project with rapidity.

FLASH DRIVE

Here's a listing of the folders I have on my flash drive and the information contained within. Obviously, each individual will sort their information to their tastes.

- I have a folder for each of my books. Each contains an array of material I used during the researching and writing process plus the actual work itself.
- I have a folder for a biographical encyclopedia that I help proof and fact check.
- I have a folder for each periodical that I download; each contains multiple issues of that periodical. For example. SABR has articles and issues of *The National Pastime* and *Baseball Research Journal* which can be downloaded. Similarly, I have quite a few articles that I downloaded from Project Muse.
- I have a folder for Baseball-fever.com, the forum I visit regularly. It contains copies of old threads and a master list of user names matched with their true names.
- I also have separate folders for my blog work, baseball pictures, various resumes, unpublished articles and published articles. Like

many, I have a My Documents folder which holds miscellaneous forms and other data.

- There is a folder titled Others' Research. It's full of various articles and information that I've accrued from others. It's not my work so I need to make sure I use and store it accordingly.
- The most active folder on my drive is a self explanatory one, titled Works in Progress.
- Another vital folder contains my notes files that are explained in the next section.

THE MS WORD NOTE FILE

One of my preferences is to pull data into a MS Word document. It is extremely quick to copy and paste from web sites and digital databases. I typically call this document by subject name and then add the word "Notes" at the end, like "Eddie Plank Notes." At the end of my search, this document could be dozens of pages long – but it's all information I didn't have to write by hand. I'll make hard copies along the way as the information builds, so at my leisure I can relax away from the computer and make my manual notes.

Use the "Snapshot Tool" with digital databases. This will permit you to pull small bits of text into your "Notes" MS Word file. My "Notes" files have dozens of small bits of old articles that are specific to my subject. I set my MS Word document at two columns - that way I can have numerous articles on one page. Some snapshots may be only a few lines of newspaper text long; others may be as long as the page itself. Some software like that used by the *Brooklyn Eagle* archive and Nineteenth Century Newspapers require that you convert to PDF form which will allow the use of the snapshot tool.

The above can also save you money on copying. One article that may be two pages long if you were to print it could be one page if you slice it into several snapshots.

Invariably while cutting and pasting from various websites, the fonts in the "Notes" file will vary. I will change all of them to Times New Roman 10. Also, the color may need to be changed, as well as, the underlining and italics and bold text. This might shrink your file by several pages and obviously be cheaper if you were to print it out.

THE OUTLINE PACKET

Now that you have all this great information, how do you make the segue to writing? Well, obviously, you have to organize your data in a desired fashion. For many topics, this means into chronological order. However, certain material may require a different approach.

Write an outline of how you want to present your story. It doesn't need to be complex. Since many stories flow chronologically, the outline tends to write itself. I usually grab a blank pad and title each page in order straight from the outline. Here's an example for an article-length biography:

- Introduction
- Early life – I usually include his birth family information here, as well as, schooling and other information.
- Early baseball – I may have separate pages here if there is significant data for amateur, semi-pro and/or college clubs.
- Then, the bulk of the piece – the professional baseball years. I'll mark one page for each year. In the case of Eddie Plank, there will be seventeen pages, 1901-1917.
- Later baseball – I may have separate pages here if there is significant data for his time umpiring, continued playing time, work as an executive, etc.
- Later life – I often include information here on his marriage family, post-baseball jobs and of course his death.

The preceding is just a guide and will fluctuate with each different subject. I may have a great deal of information for a certain period and, thus, have several pages for say 1905. Also, if I'm dealing with a pitcher, I'll have a separate section for his pitching style and plug it in where I deem appropriate.

Now I'm organized and at a position that I can start weeding through my notes and copied articles and place refined notes about them within my outline packet from above.

In truth, I make the outline packet early on and begin filling it in as soon as possible. After I've done a round of research, I read the notes and materials and place it in the outline – that way I'm not overwhelmed with a huge stack of notes at once.

Likewise, this affords me the opportunity to breakup another chore. As I'm going through my notes and materials, I'm accruing a list of sources and a stack of quotes that at some point I'll want to insert into my text. (In my notes and materials, I put Post-its to identify the quotes I want to incorporate into my work.)

So, I create the MS Word file for the project – where I'm going to write my story; it might be called "Eddie Plank Working File." After each round of research, I plug in the sources and type in the quotes. If I don't do this little by little, it can become a big job – and as we all know we often put off big jobs. Make sure to cite the quotes so you have that readily on hand. Since I write/type in black on white, I enter the quotes in blue. That way, I know very clearly that it's just floating data and not yet incorporated into the text.

Also, I may have written something previously that would fit into my Eddie Plank story and I'll want to use it, or at least a version of it. I pull this from its home file and insert it into the "Eddie Plank Working File" in green. It's my work so I'm not stealing, but I'll want to restate it or otherwise modify it later. Putting it in green lets me know that it's floating data that hasn't been incorporated into the text and that it needs tweaking.

After I've finished filling in my outline packet, and transferring the needed information into the Working File, that working file may be quite substantial already – and I haven't even started writing. There may be dozens of quotes. Make sure to put the quotes in chronological order so that everything is organized as your writing each subsequent part of the story.

REREAD YOUR NOTES AND MATERIALS

After I've read all my notes and materials and entered them in the outline, I go back and scan the information again. The reason here is that at different points throughout the process my perspective changes. Now that I accrued most of my data and read it at least once, I want to reread it because I may not have understood something when I originally read it, my overall perspective has adapted or, most of all, I may have missed or overlooked something. I also may not have understood the relevance of something I read before or tied everything together in my mind completely.

A common example of this is the following. The information you accrue is done so in a haphazard fashion. By this, I mean that you're not pulling everything in and absorbing it in a strict timeline, as you'll be presenting it. Sometimes you will find the results of X, before knowing the facts of incident X itself.

For instance, I may discover that a player is idle for three weeks in June of 1892. It may not necessarily strike me as odd at the time. But, I jot it down for later consideration. In my subsequent readings, I may find references to him being suspended or injured or whatever. I may or may not find the root cause though and I'll have to go searching if I don't.

The obvious way to do this is to track his presence in the lineup and to run searches within a strict timeframe. Some newspaper somewhere made a reference to the reason for his absence; I just have to find it. Be aware that the further you go back in time, the less you might find. The reason may be buried in a game recap somewhere and not talked about again. Just use some detective work to find it.

To get back to my point, as you read you are gathering information, let's call the pieces of information A, B, C, D, E, F, G, H, I, J, K, L, M ... and so forth. It's only later, perhaps much later, that you realize K may be tied to C, or B and J are tied to M.

Chapter Eight

WRITING AND GETTING PUBLISHED

You've done the research – the bulk of it at least – and filled in your outline packet. It's time to write your story. If you're looking for help on writing or publishing, look elsewhere. Dictionaries, thesauruses, grammar and 'getting published' guides are available elsewhere and cannot be incorporated here. I'll try to touch on some points though that hopefully will make this chapter worthwhile.

It would seem natural to write your story in order of the outline but you may choose to do it out of order. It's up to you. From the example presented in the previous chapter, I often like to write the early and later life portions of the story and then focus on the bulk of the story – the professional years. Sometimes I write the introduction at the onset of my writing, sometimes at the end.

I say, whatever spurs you to start your project the better. If you want to dive in on a particularly interesting chapter that may reside in say the middle the work, go ahead. The great benefit to a word processing program is the ability to make adjustments and move your work around, repeatedly.

However you start, make sure you pull as much of the information from the outline packet as you now find worthwhile. Not every tidbit and scrap of information will be relevant or even seem appropriate when you're actually in the mode of telling the story. I make sure to meld in the blue and green type that I inputted earlier.

I usually write with an internet window, or several, open. I'm constantly rechecking information and pulling things into the story. Don't get bogged down, bust out that chapter or section of the project. Now's the point I use my last colored font – red. I use it for:

- Anything I'm not sure about
- Anything I'm missing
- Needed data
- Data which I need to verify, fact check
- If I feel I need to restate something, or present it differently

As I progress, my work is typically littered with red text within the body of the work. In the drive to be complete and factual, you'll have to constantly verify data and seek additional information. This can weigh you down while writing. I simply make a corresponding note in red or highlight something in red. Then, I know that I need to come back and make the appropriate adjustments.

The examples here are numerous. It could be as little as verifying a name or stat or rewriting an entire paragraph because I'm just not happy with the way it came out. I also write questions – prompting me to do further research - at the beginning, middle or end of paragraphs and highlight them in red.

For instance, old newspapers typically referred to people by their last name only. If I pull such a quote, I'll have to plug in a first name. This may not always be easy if we're talking about a bunch of minor leaguers or team or league officials. Trying to find that correct name at that moment will only slow the project down. I put it in red and then set aside some time for additional research to answer all these questions. It keeps the flow going and actually keeps my mind on top of things.

Write for the common man, as if they don't know the ins and outs of baseball history. Don't refer to an incident in baseball history or an individual and assume the reader will know who or what you're talking about. Not everyone that reads your piece will be fluent in baseball history; in fact, most won't be.

Don't just mention Ban Johnson without identifying his job title and his importance in your piece and why he's important. Don't casually refer to the Black Sox of 1919 without giving at least a short description of whom or what they were. This is where proofreading, readers and editors come into play.

You may initially make these mistakes while writing, so you need to proof your work to make sure it comes across well. You may need to do this several times. Also, have friends or others read it and prompt you with questions. This will help you to better understand how your work is coming across and where it needs to be refined.

Learn to accept criticism from editors or informed readers – they may not know more about the subject you just thoroughly researched, but they may have a greater insight into how your material comes across, its readability and confusing points you may not have fully explained or developed. For instance, if they feel that you have inundated or bored them with statistics or game recaps, take that into account. These people are your audience.

This is also true with the actual writing. If that's new to you – as it was to me – you have a lot to learn about presenting your material and developing a competent and coherent style of writing. It's all in the details. Along these lines, editors are extremely helpful. The more opinions you get on your work – even critical ones – helps you present your material more efficiently and fluid in the future.

Don't worry, it will come, but it definitely helps to have a good understanding of grammar or at least to pay attention to the little red and green lines under your mistakes in MS Word.

This is obviously just a partial listing of available works.

BIOGRAPHIES AND AUTOBIOGRAPHIES

Naturally, biographies and autobiographies contain great information. Some are must reads. They are too numerous to mention and are easily stumbled upon through a simple Google search.

GENERAL HISTORY

Alexander, Charles C. *Our Game: An American Baseball History*. New York: Henry Holt and Company, 1991.

Bevis, Charlie. *Sunday Baseball: The Major Leagues' Struggle to Play Baseball on the Lord's Day, 1876-1934*. Jefferson, North Carolina: McFarland & Company, Inc., Publishers, 2003.

Bowman, John and Joel Zoss. *Diamonds in the Rough: The Untold History of Baseball.* Chicago: Contemporary Books, 1996.

Burk, Robert F. *Never Just a Game: Players, Owners, and American Baseball to 1920.* Chapel Hill, North Carolina: The University of North Carolina Press, 1994.

Burk, Robert F. *Much More Than a Game: Players, Owners, and American Baseball Since 1921.* Chapel Hill, North Carolina: University of North Carolina Press, 2001.

Dewey, Donald and Nicholas Acocella. *The New Biographical History of Baseball.* Chicago: Triumph Books, 2002.

Dewey, Donald and Nicholas Acocella. *Total Ballclubs: The Ultimate Book of Baseball Teams.* Wilmington, Delaware: Sports Media Publishing, Inc., 2005.

Dickson, Paul. *The New Dickson Baseball Dictionary.* New York: Harcourt Brace and Company, 1999.

Dreifort, John E. *Baseball History from Outside the Lines: A Reader.* Lincoln: University of Nebraska Press, 2001.

Filichia, Peter. *Professional Baseball Franchises: From the Abbeville Athletics to the Zanesville Indians.* New York: Facts On File, Inc., 1993.

Ginsburg, Daniel E. *The Fix Is In: A History of Baseball Gambling and Game-Fixing Scandals.* Jefferson, NC and London: McFarland & Company, Inc., 1995.

James, Bill. *The New Bill James Historical Baseball Abstract.* New York: The Free Press, 2001.

James, Bill and Rob Neyer. *The Neyer/James Guide to Pitchers: An Historical Compendium of Pitching, Pitchers, and Pitches.* New York: Simon and Schuster, 2004.

Kahn, Roger. *The Head Game: Baseball Seen from the Pitcher's Mound.* New York: Houghton Mifflin Harcourt, 2001.

Koppett, Leonard. *Koppett's Concise History of Major League Baseball.* Philadelphia: Temple University Press, 1998.

Lee, Bill. *The Baseball Necrology: The Post-Baseball Lives of Over 7,600 Major League Players and Others.* Jefferson, North Carolina: McFarland & Company, Inc., Publishers, 2003.

Leitner, Irving A. *Diamond in the Rough.* New York: Criterion Books, 1972.

Light, Jonathan Fraser. *The Cultural Encyclopedia of Baseball.* Jefferson, North Carolina: McFarland & Company, Inc., 1997.

Lowry, Philip J. *Green Cathedrals: The Ultimate Celebration of All 271 Major League and Negro League Ballpark Past and Present.* Reading, Massachusetts: Addison-Wesley Publishing Co., Inc., 1992.

McKenna, Brian. *Early Exits: The Premature Endings of Baseball Careers.* Lanham, Maryland: Scarecrow Press, 2006.

Mead, William B. and Paul Dickson. *Baseball The Presidents' Game.* New York: Walker and Company, 1997.

Morris, Peter. *A Game of Inches: The Stories Behind the Innovations That Shaped Baseball, The Game on the Field.* Chicago, Ivan R. Dee, 2006.

Morris, Peter. *A Game of Inches: The Stories Behind the Innovations That Shaped Baseball, The Game Behind the Scenes.* Chicago, Ivan R. Dee, 2006.

Morris, Peter. Level *Playing Fields: How the Groundskeeping Murphy Brothers Shaped Baseball.* Nebraska: University of Nebraska Press, 2007.

Nemec, David and Dave Zeman. *The Baseball Rookies Encyclopedia.* Dulles, Virginia: Brassey's, 2004.

Pietrusza, David. *Lights On!: The Wild Century-Long Saga of Night Baseball.* Lanham, Maryland: The Scarecrow Press, Inc., 1997.

Pietrusza, David, Matthew Silverman and Michael Gershman. *Baseball: The Biographical Encyclopedia.* New York: Total/Sports Illustrated, 2000.

Porter, David L. *Biographical Dictionary of American Sports: Baseball.* New York: Greenwood Press, 1987.

Rader, Benjamin G. *Baseball: A History of America's Game.* Urbana and Chicago: University of Illinois Press, 1992.

Seymour, Harold. *Baseball: The Early Years.* New York: Oxford University Press, 1960.

Seymour, Harlod. *Baseball: The Golden Age.* New York: Oxford University Press, 1971.

Seymour, Harold. *Baseball: The People's Game.* New York: Oxford University Press, 1990.

Shatzkin, Mike and Jim Carlton. *The Ballplayers: Baseball's Ultimate Biographical Reference.* New York: Arbor House, 1990.

Solomon, Burt. *The Baseball Timeline.* New York: DK Publishing, Inc., 2001.

Sullivan, Dean A. *Early Innings: A Documentary History of Baseball, 1825-1908*. Lincoln, Nebraska: University of Nebraska Press, 1995.

Sullivan, Dean A. *Middle Innings: A Documentary History of Baseball, 1900-1948*. Lincoln, Nebraska: University of Nebraska Press, 1998.

Thorn, John and Pete Palmer. *Total Baseball*. New York: Warner Books, 1989.

Thorn, John. *The Relief Pitcher: Baseball's New Hero*. New York: E.P. Dutton, 1979.

Thorn, John, Pete Palmer, Michael Gershman and David Pietrusza. *Total Baseball: The Official Encyclopedia of Major League Baseball, Sixth Edition*. New York: Total Sports, 1999.

Thorn, John, Pete Palmer, Michael Gershman. *Total Baseball: The Official Encyclopedia of Major League Baseball, Seventh Edition*. New York: Total Sports, 2001.

Thorn, John, Phil Birnbaum, Bill Deane, Rob Neyer, Alan Schwarz, Donald Dewey, Nicholas Acocella and Peter Wayner. *Total Baseball: The Ultimate Baseball Encyclopedia, Eighth Edition*. Wilmington, Delaware: Sport Classic Books, 2004.

Tygiel, Jules. *Past Time: Baseball as History*. Oxford: Oxford University Press, 2000.Voigt, David Quentin. *American Baseball: From the Commissioners to Continental Expansion, Volume II*. University Park, Pennsylvania: The Pennsylvania State University Press, 1992.

Voight, David Quentin. *American Baseball: Volume One*. University Park and London: The Pennsylvania State University Press, 1983. – Three volume set

BLACK BASEBALL

Brunson, James Edward. *The Early Image of Black Baseball: Race and Representation in the Popular Press, 1871-1890.* Jefferson, North Carolina: McFarland and Company, 2009.

Clark, Dick and Larry Lester. *The Negro Leagues Book.* Cleveland, Ohio: Society for American Baseball Research, 1994.

Dixon, Phil and Patrick J. Hannigan. *The Negro Leagues: A Photographic History.* New York: Amereon House, 1992.

Heaphy, Leslie A. *The Negro Leagues, 1869-1960.* Jefferson, North Carolina: McFarland and Company, 2003.

Hoffbeck, Stephen R. *Swing for the Fences: Black Baseball in Minnesota.* St. Paul: Minnesota Historical Society, 2005.

Hogan, Lawrence D. *Shades of Glory: The Negro Leagues and the Story of African-American Baseball.* Washington D.C.: National Geographic, 2006.

Holway, John B. *Blackball Stars: Negro League Stars.* Westport, CT: Meckler Books, 1988.

Holway, John B. *Black Diamonds: Life in the Negro Leagues from the Men Who Lived It.* Westport, Connecticut: Meckler Books, 1989.

Holway, John. *The Complete Book of Baseball's Negro Leagues: The Other Half of Baseball History.* Fern Park, Florida: Hastings House Publishers, 2001.

Kelley, Brent. *The Negro Leagues Revisited: Conversations with 66 More Baseball Heroes.* Jefferson, NC: McFarland & Company, Inc., Publishers, 2000.

Kirsch, George B., Othello Harris and Claire Elaine Nolte. *Encyclopedia of Ethnicity and Sports in the United States.* Westport, Connecticut: Greenwood Publishing Group, 2000.

Kirwin, Bill. *Out of the Shadows: African American Baseball from the Cuban Giants to Jackie Robinson.* Lincoln: University of Nebraska Press, 2005.

Lanctot, Neil. *Fair Dealing and Clean Playing: The Hilldale Club and the Development of Black Professional Baseball, 1910-1932.* Jefferson, NC: McFarland & Company, 1994.

Lanctot, Neil. *Negro League Baseball: The Rise and Ruin of a Black Institution.* Philadelphia: University of Pennsylvania Press, 2004.

Lomax, Michael E. *Black Baseball Entrepreneurs, 1860-1901: Operating by Any Means Necessary.* Syracuse, New York: Syracuse University Press, 2003.

Malloy, Jerry. *Sol White's History of Colored Base Ball With Other Documents on the Early Black Game 1886-1936.* Lincoln: University of Nebraska Press, 1995.

Martin, Alfred M. and Alfred T. Martin. *The Negro Leagues in New Jersey: A History.* Jefferson, North Carolina: McFarland and Company, 2008.

McKissack, Patricia C. and Frederick McKissack, Jr. *Black Diamond: The Story of the Negro Baseball Leagues.* New York: Scholastic, Inc., 1994.

McNeil, William F. *Baseball's Other All-Stars.* Jefferson, North Carolina: McFarland & Company, Inc., Publishers, 2000.

Peterson, Robert. *Only the Ball was White: A History of Legendary Black Players and All-Black Professional Teams Before Black Men Played in the Major Leagues.* New York: McGraw-Hill Book Co., 1970.

Ribowsky, Mark. *A Complete History of the Negro Leagues 1884-1955.* New York: Citadel Press Books, 2002.

Riley, James A. *The Biographical Encyclopedia of the Negro Baseball Leagues.* New York: Carroll and Graf Publishers, 1994.

Rogosin, Donn. *Invisible Men: Life in Baseball's Negro Leagues.* New York: MacMillan Publishing Co., 1983.

Ruck, Rob. *Sandlot Seasons: Sport in Black Pittsburgh.* Illinois: University of Illinois Press, 1993.

Snyder, Brad. *Beyond the Shadow of the Senator: The Untold Story of the Homestead Grays and the Integration of Baseball.* Chicago: Contemporary Books, 2003.

Society for American Baseball Research. *The SABR Baseball List and Record Book.* New York: SABR, 2007.

INTERNATIONAL BASEBALL

Bauer, Carlos. *The All-Time Japanese Baseball Register: The Complete Statistical Record of All the Great Japanese and American Players.* San Diego: Baseball Press Books, 2000.

Bjarkman, Peter C. *Diamonds Around the Globe: The Encyclopedia of International Baseball.* Westport, Connecticut: Greenwood Press, 2005.

Burgos Jr., Adrian. *Playing America's Game: Baseball, Latinos, and the Color Line.* Berkeley, California: University of California Press, 2007.

Clark, Joe. *A History of Australian Baseball: Time and Game.* Lincoln, Nebraska: University of Nebraska Press, 2003.

Echevarria, Roberto Gonzalez. The Pride of Havana: A History of Cuban Baseball. New York: Oxford University Press, 1999.

Figueredo, Jorge S. *Cuban Baseball: A Statistical History, 1878-1961.* Jefferson, North Carolina: McFarland and Company, 2003.

Finnan, Jane. *Dominionball: Baseball Above the 49th*. Cleveland, Ohio: Society for American Baseball Research, 2005.

Fitts, Robert K. *Remembering Japanese Baseball: An Oral History of the Game*. Illinois: Southern Illinois University Press, 2005.

Gonzalez Echevarria, Roberto. *The Pride of Havana: A History of Cuban Baseball*. New York: Oxford University Press, 1999.

Humber, William. *Diamonds of the North: A Concise History of Baseball in Canada*. Toronto: Oxford University Press, 1995.

Humber, William and Spider Jones. *A Sporting Chance: Achievements of African-Canadian Athletes*. Toronto, Ontario, Canada: Dundurn Press Ltd., 2004.

Johnson, Daniel E. *Japanese Baseball: A Statistical Handbook*. Jefferson, North Carolina: McFarland & Company, Inc., Publishers, 1999.

Oleksak, Michael M. and Mary Adams Oleksak. *Latin Americans and the Grand Old Game*. Grand Rapids, Michigan: Masters Press, 1991.

Reaves, Joseph A. *Taking in a Game: A History of Baseball in Asia*. Lincoln, Nebraska: University of Nebraska Press, 2002.

Regalado, Samuel Octavio. *Viva Baseball: Latin Major Leaguers and their Special Hunger*. Urbana and Chicago: University of Illinois Press, 1998.

Ruck, Rob. *The Tropic of Baseball: Baseball in the Dominican Republic*. Lincoln: University of Nebraska Press, 1999.

Whiting, Robert. *The Chrysanthemum and the Bat: The Game Japanese Play*. Tokyo, Japan: The Permanent Press, 1977.

Whiting, Robert. *The Samurai Way of Baseball: The Impact of Ichiro and the New Wave from Japan*. New York: Time Warner Book Group, 2004.

Wilson, Nick C. *Early Latino Ballplayers in the United States: Major, Minor and Negro Leagues, 1901-1949*. Jefferson, North Carolina: McFarland & Company, Inc., Publishers, 2005.

NINETEENTH CENTURY

Alvarez, Mark. *The Old Ball Game: Baseball's Beginnings*. Alexandria, VA: Redefinition, 1990.

Goldstein, William. *A History of Early Baseball*. New York: Barnes and Noble, 2000.

Ivor-Campbell, Frederick, Robert L. Tiemann and Mark Rucker. *Baseball's First Stars*. Cleveland: The Society for American Baseball Research, 1996.

Kirsch, George B. *Baseball in Blue and Gray: The National Pastime during the Civil War*. Princeton, New Jersey: Princeton University Press, 2003.

Lamster, Mark. *Spalding's World Tour: The Epic Adventure That Took Baseball Around the Globe and Made it America's Game*. New York: Public Affairs, 2006.

Melville, Tom. *Early Baseball and the Rise of the National League*. Jefferson, North Carolina: McFarland & Company, 2001.

Morris, Peter. *But Didn't We Have Fun?: An Informal History of Baseball's Pioneer Era, 1843-1870*. Chicago: Ivan R. Dee, 2008.

Morris, Peter. *Catcher: How the Man Behind the Plate Became an American Folk Hero*. Chicago, Ivan R. Dee, 2009.

Nemec, David. *The Beer and Whiskey League: The Illustrated History of the American Association - Baseball's Renegade Major League.* New York: Lyons and Burford, Publishers, 1994.

Nemec, David. *The Great Encyclopedia of 19th Century Major League Baseball.* New York: Donald I. Fine Books, 1997.

Pearson, Daniel Merle. *Baseball in 1889: Players vs. Owners.* Wisconsin: Popular Press, 1993.

Ryczek, William J. *Blackguards and Red Stockings: A History of Baseball's National Association, 1871-1875.* Wallingford, Connecticut: Colebrook Press, 1992.

Ryczek, William J. *When Johnny Came Sliding Home: The Post-Civil War Baseball Boom, 1865-1870.* Jefferson, North Carolina: McFarland & Company, Inc., Publishers, 1998.

Ryczek, William J. *Baseball's First Inning: A History of the National Pastime through the Civil War.* Jefferson, North Carolina: McFarland & Company, 2009.

Schwarz, Alan. *The Numbers Game: Baseball's Lifelong Fascination with Statistics.* New York: St. Martin's Press, 2004.

Spalding, Albert G. *America's National Game.* Lincoln and London: University of Nebraska Press, 1992.

Tiemann, Robert L. and Mark Rucker. *Nineteenth Century Stars.* Cleveland: Society for American Baseball Research, 1989.

Wright, Marshall D. *The National Association of Base Ball Players, 1857-1870.* Jefferson, NC: McFarland & Company, 2000.

FEMALE BASEBALL

Ardell, Jean Hastings. *Breaking into Baseball: Women and the National Pastime.* Carbondale: Southern Illinois University Press, 2005.

Gregorich, Barbara. *Women at Play: The Story of Women in Baseball.* San Diego: Harcourt Brace and Company, 1993.

Madden, W. C. *The Women of the All-American Girls Professional Baseball League: A Biographical Dictionary.* Jefferson, North Carolina: McFarland & Company, Inc., 1997.

Madden, W. C. *The All-American Girls Professional Baseball League Record Book: Comprehensive Hitting, Fielding and Pitching Statistics.* Jefferson, North Carolina: McFarland & Company, Inc., 2000.

Markel, Robert, Susan Waggoner and Marcella Smith. *The Women's Sports Encyclopedia: The Comprehensive Guide to Women's Sports, Women Athletes, and their Records.* New York: Henry Holt and Company, 1997.

MINOR LEAGUE BASEBALL

Johnson, Lloyd. *The Minor League Register.* Durham, North Carolina: Baseball America, Inc., 1994.

Johnson, Lloyd and Miles Wolff. *The Encyclopedia of Minor League Baseball, Second Edition.* Durham, North Carolina: Baseball America, Inc., 1997.

McNeil, William. *The California Winter League: America's First Integrated Professional Baseball League.* Jefferson, North Carolina: McFarland & Company, 2002.

Nelson, Kevin. *The Golden Game: The Story of California Baseball.* San Francisco: California Historical Society Press, 2004.

Obojski, Robert. *Bush League: A History of Minor League Baseball.* New York: Macmillan Publishing Co., Inc., 1975.

O'Neal, Bill. *The Texas League 1888-1987: A Century of Baseball.* Austin, Texas: Eakin Press, 1987.

O'Neal, Bill. *The Pacific Coast League: 1903-1988.* Austin, Texas: Eakin Press, 1990.

O'Neal, Bill. *The International League: A Baseball History, 1884-1991.* Austin, Texas: Eakin Press, 1992.

O'Neal, Bill. *The Southern League: Baseball in Dixie, 1885-1994.* Austin, Texas: Eakin Press, 1994.

Spalding, John E. *Always on Sunday: The California Baseball League, 1886 to 1915.* Manhattan, Kansas: Ag Press, 1992.

Sullivan, Neil J. *The Minors: The Struggles and the Triumph of Baseball's Poor Relation From 1876 to the Present.* New York: St. Martin's Press, 1990.

Utley, R.G. and Scott Verner. *The Independent Carolina Baseball League, 1936-1938:*
Baseball Outlaws. Jefferson, NC: McFarland & Company, 1999.

Wright, Marshall D. *The International League: Year-by-Year Statistics, 1884-1953.* Jefferson, NC: McFarland & Company, Inc., Publishers, 1998.

Zingg, Paul J. and Mark D. Medeiros. *Runs, Hits, and an Era: The Pacific Coast League, 1903-58.* Illinois: University of Illinois Press, 1994.

TEAM-RELATED PIECES

Caruso, Gary. *The Braves Encyclopedia.* Philadelphia: Temple University Press, 1995.

Cash, Jon David. *Before They Were Cardinals: Major League Baseball in Nineteenth-century St. Louis.* University of St. Louis Press, 2002.

Debano, Paul. *The Indianapolis ABCs: History of a Premier Team in the Negro Leagues.* Jefferson, North Carolina: McFarland & Company, 1997.

Deford, Frank. *The Old Ball Game: How John McGraw, Christy Mathewson, and the New York Giants created Modern Baseball.* New York: Atlantic Monthly Press, 2005.

Deveaux, Tom. *The Washington Senators, 1901-1971.* Jefferson, North Carolina: McFarland & Company, Inc., Publishers, 2001.

Egan, James M. Jr. *Baseball on the Western Reserve: The Early Game in Cleveland and Northeast Ohio, Year by Year and Town by Town 1865-1900.* Jefferson, North Carolina: McFarland & Company, 2008.

Ellard, Henry. *Baseball in Cincinnati: A History.* Jefferson, North Carolina: McFarland & Company, 2004.

Felber, Bill. *A Game of Brawl: The Orioles, the Beaneaters and the Battle for the 1897 Pennant.* Lincoln, Nebraska: University of Nebraska Press, 2007.

Frommer, Frederic J. *The Washington Nationals 1849 to Today.* Lanham, MD: First Taylor Trade Publishing, 2006.

Gentile, Derek. *The Complete Chicago Cubs: The Total Encyclopedia of the Team.* New York: Black Dog & Leventhal, 2004.

Golenbock, Peter. *Wrigleyville: A Magical History Tour of the Chicago Cubs.* New York: St. Martin's Griffin, 1999.

Guschov, Stephen D. *The Red Stockings of Cincinnati: Base Ball's First All-professional Team and its Historic 1869 and 1870 Seasons.* Jefferson, North Carolina: McFarland & Company, 1998.

Halberstam, David. Read by Edwin Newman. *October 1964.* New York: Random   House Audio Books, 1994.

Hardy, James D., Jr. *The New York Giants Base Ball Club: The Growth of a Team and a Sport, 1870-1900.* Jefferson, North Carolina: McFarland & Company, Inc., Publishers, 1996.

Hetrick, J. Thomas. *Chris von der Ahe and the St. Louis Browns.* Lanham, Maryland: Rowan and Littlefield, 1999.

Kaese, Harold. *The Boston Braves: 1871-1953.* University Press of New England, 2004.

Lewis, Franklin A. *The Cleveland Indians.* Kent, Ohio: Kent State University Press, 2006.

Lieb, Frederick G. *The Baltimore Orioles: The History of a Colorful Team in Baltimore and St. Louis.* Carbondale: Southern Illinois University Press, 1955.

McBane, Richard. *A Fine-looking Lot of Ball Tossers: The Remarkable Akrons of 1881.* Jefferson, NC: McFarland & Company, 2005.

Morris, Peter. *Baseball Fever: Early Baseball in Michigan.* Ann Arbor, Michigan: University of Michigan Press, 2003.

Podoll, Brian A. *The Minor League Milwaukee Brewers 1859-1952.* Jefferson, North Carolina: McFarland & Company, Inc., Publishers, 2003.

Povich, Shirley. *The Washington Senators: An Informal History.* New York: G.P. Putnam's Sons, 1954.

Schneider, Russell. *Cleveland Indians Encyclopedia: 2nd Edition.* Illinois: Sports Publishing LLC, 2001.

Solomon, Burt. *Where They Ain't: The Fabled Life and Untimely Death of the Original Baltimore Orioles. The Team that Gave Birth to Modern Baseball.* New York: Doubleday Books, 1999.

Stout, Glenn. *Yankees Century: 100 Years of New York Yankees Baseball.* New York: Houghton Mifflin Company, 2002.

Terry, James L. *Long Before the Dodgers: Baseball in Brooklyn, 1855-1884.* Jefferson, North Carolina: McFarland & Company, 2002.

Thornley, Stew. *Baseball in Minnesota: A Definitive History.* St. Paul: Minnesota Historical Society, 2006.

Tofel, Richard J. *A Legend in the Making: The New York Yankees in 1939.* Chicago: Ivan R. Dee, 2002.

PERIOD PIECES

Alexander, Charles C. *Breaking the Slump: Baseball in the Depression Era.* New York: Columbia University Press, 2002.

Bloomfield, Gary. *Duty, Honor, Victory: America's Athletes in World War II.* Guilford, Connecticut: The Lyons Press, 2003.

Browning, Reed. *Baseball's Greatest Season: 1924.* Boston: University of Massachusetts Press, 2003.

Bryant, Howard. *Juicing the Game: Drugs, Power, and the Fight for the Soul of Major League Baseball.* New York: Penguin Group, 2005.

Cox, James A. *The Lively Ball: Baseball in the Roaring Twenties.* Alexandria, Virginia: Redefinition, 1989.

Creamer, Robert W. *Baseball in '41.* Ashland, Oregon: Blackstone Audiobooks, 1997.

Jones, David. *Deadball Stars of the American League.* Dulles, Virginia: Potomac Books, Inc., 2006.

Mead, William B. *Low and Outside: Baseball in the Depression, 1930-1939.* Alexandria, Virginia: Redefinition, Inc., 1990.

Mead, William B. *Baseball Goes to War: Stars Don Khaki, 4-Fs Vie for Pennant.* Washington D.C.: Broadcast Interview Source, Inc., 1998.

Okkonen, Marc. *The Federal League of 1914-15: Baseball's Third Major League.* Garrett Park, MD: Society for American Baseball Research, 1989.

Pepe, Phil. *Talkin' Baseball: An Oral History of Baseball in the 1970s.* New York: Ballantine Publishing Group, 1998.

Reisler, Jim. *A Great Day in Cooperstown: The Improbable Birth of Baseball's Hall of Fame.* New York: Carroll & Graf Publishers, 2006.

Riess, Steven A. *Touching Base: Professional Baseball and American Culture in the Progressive Era, Second Edition.* Illinois: University of Illinois Press, 1999.

Sowell, Mike. *The Pitch That Killed: Carl Mays, Ray Chapman and the Pennant Race of 1920.* New York: MacMillan Publishing Company, 1989.

Stark, Benton. *The Year They Called Off the World Series.* New York: Avery Publishing Group Inc., 1991.

Turner, Frederick. *When the Boys Came Back: Baseball and 1946.* New York: Henry Holt and Company, 1996.

BUSINESS OF BASEBALL

Abrams, Roger I. *Legal Bases: Baseball and the Law.* Philadelphia: Temple University Press, 1998.

Boxerman, Burton A. and Benita W. Boxerman. *Ebbets to Veeck to Busch: Eight Owners Who Shaped Baseball.* Jefferson, North Carolina: McFarland & Company, Inc., Publishers, 2003.

Helyar, John. *Lords of the Realm: The Real History of Baseball.* New York: Villard

Books, 1994.

Holtzman, Jerome. *The Commissioners: Baseball's Midlife Crisis.* New York: Total Sports, 1998.

Honig, Donald. *Baseball Between the Lines: Baseball in the Forties and Fifties as Told by the Men Who Played It.* Nebraska: University of Nebraska Press, 1993.

Korr, Charles P. *The End of Baseball As We Knew It: The Players Union, 1960-81.* Urbana and Chicago: University of Illinois Press, 2002.

Lewis, Michael. *Moneyball: The Art of Winning an Unfair Game.* New York: W.W. Norton & Company, 2003.

McKelvey, G. Richard. *The MacPhails: Baseball's First Family of the Front Office.* Jefferson, North Carolina: McFarland & Company, 2000.

Miller, Marvin. *A Whole Different Ballgame: The Sport and Business of Baseball.* New York: Carol Publishing Group, 1991.

Powers, Albert Theodore. *The Business of Baseball.* Jefferson, NC: McFarland &

Company, Inc., Publishers, 2003.

Staudohar, Paul D. *Diamond Mines: Baseball and Labor.* New York: Syracuse University Press, 2000.

Zimbalist, Andrew. *Baseball and Billions: A Probing Look Inside the Big Business of Our National Pastime.* New York: Basic Books, 1994.

Zimbalist, Andrew. *In the Best Interest of Baseball?: The Revolutionary Reign of Bud Selig.* Hoboken, New Jersey: John Wiley & Sons, 2006.

Appendix B: Resource Checklist

Next, you'll find my "Resource Checklist." It's nothing awe-inspiring but it keeps me organized. Some of the listed entries won't make sense to you; it's a personal sheet I use, so I know that I have examined the resources that I've found most useful and didn't forget anything. I didn't make it for publication, so there is no thought behind it to polish it for others; it's just something I use.

I print out a new one for each subject I start to research. (I don't print out a bunch of them because I'm constantly updating and tweaking it.) Basically, it's just a checklist of resources. Make your own and utilize it as you please.

I cross off the items after I've utilized them. That's self explanatory. After hitting the web sites or other sources and pulling information off them, I scratch until the resources are depleted. Any special books, articles or other sources I need to examine that are subject-specific. I handwrite on the front or the back.

Some points:

- "My Accrued Research Notes" – This just reminds me that I've done a lot of research in the past and may have valuable information in another file. For example, I did research on Hoss Radbourn. When I was later searching for info on catchers Sandy Nava and Barney Gilligan, I went to my research notes for Radbourn and my written bio of him.
- "Peter Morris Newspaper Dbs" – On his site – Petermorrisbooks.com – he has list of digital archive sites. I usually access them through his site.
- "Wikipedia Online NP Archives" – same premise as above
- "Local Contacts" – Just a list of individuals I think might be able to add something to my project. For example, when I need minor league stats, there is an individual I usually contact for assistance. Also, if I research a player that went to college, I make sure to contact the archivist at that college or university.
- NP = newspapers
- Db = database

SUBJECT

GOOGLE.COM
BOOKS.GOOGLE.COM
RETROSHEET.ORG
MY ACCRUED RESEARCH NOTES

BASEBALL-REFERENCE
☐ MINORS

SABR
☐ SABRWEBS.COM
☐ BIOGRAPHY PROJECT
☐ COLLEGE INDEX
☐ MILITARY INDEX
☐ ENCYCLOPEDIA
☐ INDEX
☐ PAPER OF RECORD
☐ *THE SPORTING NEWS*
☐ *BASEBALL RESEARCH JOURNAL*
☐ *THE NATIONAL PASTIME*

GENEALOGY SOURCES
☐ ANCESTRY.COM
☐ HERTITAGE QUEST
☐ FAMILYSEARCH.COM

LA84 FOUNDATION
☐ *BASEBALL MAGAZINE*
☐ *OUTING MAGAZINE*
☐ *SPORTING LIFE*

MID CONTINENT LIBRARY
☐ HISTORICAL NEWSPAPERS
☐ NEWSPAPER ARCHIVE
☐ 19TH CENTURY PAPERS

OTHER NEWSPAPERS
☐ *BROOKLYN EAGLE*
☐ *BALTIMORE SUN*
☐ *BALTIMORE AFRO-AMERICAN*
☐ PETER MORRIS NEWSPAPER DBS
☐ ANCESTRY.COM NEWSPAPERS
☐ WIKIPEDIA ONLINE NP ARCHIVES
☐ PAPER OF RECORD NEWSPAPERS

HALL OF FAME FILE

WEB SITES TO KEEP IN MIND
☐ MINOR LG RESEARCHER
☐ NYPL DIGITAL GALLERY
☐ BASEBALL IN WARTIME
☐ *MARQUIS WHO'S WHO*
☐ JAPANESE BASEBALL.COM
☐ FINDAGRAVE.COM
☐ AGATE TYPE WEB SITE
☐ THEDEADBALLERA.COM
☐ BASEBALL-FEVER
☐ BASEBALLLIBRARY.COM

LIBRARY DATABASES
☐ MY PERSONAL LIBRARY
☐ BALTIMORE COUNTY
☐ BALTIMORE CITY
☐ TOWSON UNIVERSITY
☐ LOYOLA/NOTRE DAME COLLEGE

NINE AND OTHER PERIODICALS

LOCAL CONTACTS
☐ LIBRARIANS
☐ ARCHIVISTS
☐ HISTORIANS

OTHER SOURCES LISTED ON BACK

Appendix C: Dates with Team

Next is something I weakly call my "Dates with Team" sheet. It's particularly helpful with players who jump around between clubs.

In any given season, a player may play for multiple teams. Say I'm looking at Player X in 1891 and he played for three different teams. Going into the project, I may have no idea when specifically he played with each team during 1891. Baseball-reference.com and Retrosheet.org might help a little if his debut or final date in the majors may have occurred in 1891, but otherwise I'm on my own.

As I come across X in newspaper searches, in box scores or in a narrative, I write the date down with the corresponding team. I use "Early Dates" and "Late Dates" just to keep it a little clean. After researching the entire year and charting the dates, I have a pretty good idea of his year. I have a timeline of that season and his movements. Make sure to note hard evidence such as an article that says something to the effect of, "This was his first game with Team C." It's always nice to say that X joined C on July 28, rather than X joined C at the end of July. Being specific and factual gives your work legitimacy.

Another benefit to charting dates is that you find errors –and can correct them in your work, creating more legitimacy. For example, you may have previously read that X was a great help for Team B in 1891 during the pennant run. Well, your research clearly shows that he was gone and done with B before the end of July. He wasn't there for the pennant run.

Even Brooks Robinson who played with one major league club for 23 seasons needs to be charted at some point. From 1955-1959, he was in and out of the majors. Identifying when and where – specifically – strengthens your work. It also helps with individuals that are injury prone – off and on the disabled list.

PLAYER:_____

YEAR/TEAM

EARLY DATES:	LATE DATES:
NOTE	

YEAR/TEAM

EARLY DATES:	LATE DATES:
NOTE	

YEAR/TEAM

EARLY DATES:	LATE DATES:
NOTE	